THE ISLAND SERIES

COLONSAY
AND ORONSAY

COLONSAY
AND ORONSAY

NORMAN S. NEWTON

David & Charles
Newton Abbot London

For Kevin and Christa

British Library Cataloguing in Publication Data

Newton, Norman S. *1944–*
 Colonsay and Oronsay.
 1.Scotland. Strathclyde Region. Colonsay & Oronsay
 I. Title
 941.4'23

 ISBN 0–7153–9239–5

Printed in Great Britain
by Redwood Press Ltd., Melksham, Wilts
for David & Charles Publishers plc
Brunel House   Newton Abbot   Devon

CONTENTS

ACKNOWLEDGEMENTS

This work would have been much more difficult without the benefit of the researches of previous writers, among whom John de Vere Loder, Baron Wakehurst, is paramount. My debt to his high standards of scholarship and the thoroughness of his investigations is gratefully acknowledged.

I would like to thank Kevin and Christa Byrne of the Isle of Colonsay Hotel for their hospitality, but especially for making available to me their collection of books and papers; John and Pamela Clarke of Milbuie, for help with the natural history of the islands; Murdo MacDonald, Argyll & Bute district archivist, for drawing my attention to items of interest; Donald MacNeill of Garvard, for the inspiration of his music and songs; Lord Strathcona and Mount Royal, for his courtesy and co-operation; and Alison Todd, branch librarian of Campbeltown Public Library, and her staff, for assistance in tracing material, frequently at short notice.

The work of the Royal Commission on the Ancient and Historical Monuments of Scotland is authoritative and my debt to its expertise is gratefully acknowledged. My thanks also for permission to use photographs from its archives.

My thanks to Sue Anderson of the island of Coll for her excellent jacket photographs, and for her advice and assistance.

Most of all, I thank the people of Colonsay and Oronsay for their unfailing courtesy and patience, and their willingness to answer all my questions.

1 FIRST IMPRESSIONS

The islands of Colonsay and Oronsay lie on the fringes of the Atlantic Ocean, twenty miles out from the mainland of Scotland. Their inhabitants form a complex, vibrant community, surviving in a landscape which can be both desperately demanding and breathtakingly magical.

Kiloran Bay, on the north-west coast of Colonsay, has a well deserved reputation as one of the finest stretches of unspoiled sand anywhere in the Hebrides. Rarely equalled, it is surely unsurpassed anywhere for its spectacular setting. In storm conditions the frightening power of the Atlantic rollers is almost overwhelming, whilst on a calm, hot day in May or September the pristine whiteness of the sand and the blueness of the sea combine to create an atmosphere of peacefulness and tranquillity much sought after by visitors from afar.

For those looking for peace and quiet, and a break from urban life and its responsibilities, there is no better place. However, the more active visitor will find plenty to do and lots of interest to investigate. Birdwatchers should be able to see fifty species in a day without straying more than a few steps from roads and tracks, while more energetic and experienced ornithologists should be able to log between seventy and eighty species in a short visit: the full list of recorded species exceeds two hundred.

Those with an interest in archaeology and history will find Colonsay and Oronsay rich and rewarding in antiquities and ruins; all periods of prehistory are represented, while the medieval remains of Oronsay Priory and the houses at Riasg Buidhe, abandoned within living memory, are evocative reminders of the islands' past. Descendants of MacPhees and

MacNeills who left Colonsay for a better life overseas will find many sites to visit on what, to many of them, will be almost an ancestral pilgrimage.

Naturalists will be astonished at the range of habitats; 600 species of local flora have been recorded. Horticulturalists and amateur gardeners will enjoy the tamed landscapes around Colonsay House. The range of animal species is more limited – there are no ground predators and no snakes in the islands – but the wild goats of Balnahard and Oronsay are interesting; according to legend they are descended from survivors of the Spanish Armada of 1588. Geologists will revel in the diversity of rocks, from the ancient gneiss of Balnahard to the Tertiary dykes of Kiloran.

The declining population of fewer than 120 live in the three small villages of Scalasaig and Upper and Lower Kilchattan, or scattered around the islands in seventeen farms and crofts, stocked with 500 cattle and 7,000 sheep. A far cry from 1841, when Colonsay and Oronsay were home to 979 islanders.

Colonsay is just over 13.5km (8 miles) in length, with a maximum breadth of 5km (3 miles). Oronsay, which lies just to the south of Colonsay, and is separated from it only at high tide, measures 2.25km (1½ miles) from north to south and 4km (2½ miles) from east to west. The islands trend NE–SW: Colonsay was sometimes called descriptively in Gaelic 'Eilean Tarsuing' – the cross-lying island. Together the islands occupy about 44sq km (17sq miles) or 4,400 hectares (10,400 acres). At a latitude of 56°08′N, the village of Scalasaig lies about as far north as Stirling, and a little further west than Land's End, at longitude 6°15′W.

Viewed from Beinn nan Gudairean (136m/446ft) situated more or less in the middle of Colonsay, above Scalasaig, the whole extent of the islands form a spectacular arc of scenery. Far off in the north-west, the island of Tiręe can sometimes be seen, a sliver on the horizon, 60km (37 miles) distant. It is best seen at midsummer, silhouetted by the setting sun. At night the light from Skerryvore lighthouse is often visible, 18.5km (11 miles) south-west of Tiree. Due north of Colonsay, 20km (12 miles) away, is the Ross of Mull, the southern peninsula of the island of Mull, with Iona at its western end. The mountains of Mull, with Ben More prominent, lie on the north-eastern horizon. The gap made by the Firth of Lorn is easily identified; this is the sea-lane used by the ferry from Oban, a lifeline 58km (36 miles) and 2½ hours long.

To the east of Colonsay is the island of Jura, with the smaller island of Scarba off its northern tip. Between Scarba and Jura is the famous whirlpool of Corryvreckan. The Paps of Jura dominate the horizon to the south-east of Colonsay, their silhouette forming a mirror image of the profile seen from the mainland, and a familiar sight from countless post-cards and calendars. The nearest point of Jura is only just over 15km (9 miles) from Scalasaig; in past centuries there was frequent contact with Jura and, of course, with Islay.

The north coast of Islay is only 9km (5½ miles) from the south tip of Oronsay, while the sea journey from Scalasaig in Colonsay to the harbour of Port Askaig in Islay is 25km (16 miles). To the south-west of Colonsay can be seen the entrance of Loch Gruinart, Ardnave Point, and the Rinns of Islay, with the mountains of Donegal in Northern Ireland visible only occasionally, 120km (75 miles) distant. So far, Colonsay and Oronsay have seemed protected, guarded and encircled by their neighbours, but face due west and feelings of emptiness, vulnerability and exposure are unavoidable; the vast expanse of the North Atlantic is unbroken for more than 3,700km (2,200 miles), except for the lonely lighthouse on Dubh Artach (sometimes spelled Du Hirteach) 30 km (19 miles) out in the ocean.

GETTING THERE AND GETTING AROUND

Visitors without a helicopter or a private yacht will arrive at Scalasaig Pier on Colonsay on one of the car ferries operated by Caledonian MacBrayne. Before a pier was built in 1965, at a cost of £150,000, passengers had to be transferred to a small boat. There is a certain amount of informal coming and going between Colonsay and Islay by local fishermen, but this mode of transport assumes access to local networks of family and friends not available to the ordinary holidaymaker. Calmac ferries sail from Oban to Colonsay; the trip takes about two and a half hours. In 1989 the company introduced a seasonal, additional, service from Kennacraig in Kintyre to Scalasaig in Colonsay, by way of Port Askaig in Islay, continuing on to Oban and returning to Kennacraig the same day. Special fares may be available under Calmac's 'Island Hopscotch' promotion. Intending travellers should contact the Calmac Offices in Oban (tel Oban (0631) 62285) or Kennacraig (tel Whitehouse (088073) 253) for the latest information on ferry timetables. The hotel proprietor and other providers of accommodation can also advise on travel arrangements.

Once in Colonsay, transport options are rather limited, but on a small island, this is not really a problem. Visitors in a hurry, or with limited mobility caused by age, infirmity, or small children, can take their cars. It is essential to make bookings for the ferry well in advance – both ways! Bicycles are available for guests at the hotel in Scalasaig and, subject to availability, can be hired by non-residents. It is possible to hire a car or an 18-seat bus on the island; enquire locally for further details. Colonsay is perfect for a walking holiday, and it is usually possible to cadge a lift at the end of a tiring day.

Accommodation is also rather limited, though there is more choice now than ever before. Apart from the well appointed hotel in Scalasaig, there are about twenty-five self-catering units available, and half-a-dozen local residents do bed and breakfast at reasonable rates. There are also now a few caravans. Details may be obtained from the Tourist Information Centre in Oban (tel Oban (0631) 63122), which can also supply a range of maps, guides and leaflets. Camping, caravans and 'camper' vans are all prohibited by the owner of Colonsay and this ban is strictly enforced.

No visit to Colonsay and Oronsay would be as enjoyable

without the advantage of a good, up-to-date map to guide the traveller's footsteps to some of the less obvious nooks and crannies of the two islands. By far the best map available is that published by the Ordnance Survey in the 'Pathfinder' series. Colonsay and Oronsay fit comfortably on to one sheet (Sheet NR 38/39/49) and the scale of 1:25,000 (2½in to one mile) is just right for exploring by car or bicycle, or on foot. The OS 'Landranger' map for Colonsay and Oronsay (Sheet 61) also includes parts of Jura and Islay, but the scale of 1:50,000 (1¼in to one mile) does not really provide enough detail to be useful, except as a general guide to the topography. One of the tourist leaflets opens up to give a good sketch map of the islands at a scale of 2in to one mile, and is a useful alternative if OS maps are unavailable. For an appreciation of Colonsay and Oronsay in a larger context, the map of Islay, Kintyre, Jura and Colonsay published by Bartholomew in their 'National' map series (Sheet 43; 1:100,000) or the OS 'Routemaster' map of Western & Central Scotland (Sheet 3; 1:250,000) is worth having. In this book, archaeological and historical sites, and some natural features of interest, are given a six figure National Grid Reference, prefixed with the letters NR: for example, Dùn Eibhinn (NR382944); Oronsay Priory (NR349889).

All in all, a successful visit to Colonsay requires a fair amount of forward planning. From May to September, the island's accommodation resources are fully stretched, and it would be extremely inadvisable to go there without a firm booking. When travelling during winter months, one should be aware of the possibility of being unavoidably detained on the island for longer than intended, due to ferry cancellations in stormy weather. In these circumstances, there is nothing for it but to make the best of an enforced extension to your holiday, and reflect on the fact that nobody is indispensable. It is to be hoped that the advent of bigger, more powerful boats on the Oban-Colonsay route will make this less common in the future. As with any Hebridean holiday, it is axiomatic that visitors should come equipped with adequate wet weather gear.

As the ferry approaches Scalasaig from Oban, it is interesting to pick out Eilean Olmsa. According to local tradition, this little island is where Bonnie Prince Charlie made his first Scottish landfall. A detailed account will be given in chapter 8. Also visible from the ferry is the deserted township of Riasg Buidhe, abandoned within living memory. However, in general the eastern coastline of Colonsay is featureless and rather unprepossessing when viewed from the sea. The same could be said of some of the neighbouring islands – the storm-shaped western coasts have the more spectacular coastal scenery.

After settling in to holiday accommodation, whether self-catering or in the luxury of the Colonsay Hotel (tel Colonsay (09512) 316), it is time for the visitor to undertake a quick orientating tour of the islands and, since most visitors will be arriving in Scalasaig (and as it is the focal point of the island, and the location of the only bar, shop and post office), it seems logical to start an introductory tour from that point.

The pier at Scalasaig is modern and has recently been further improved to accommodate the latest Calmac roll on–roll off ferries. Prominent on a hill just above the harbour to the south is a monument to Lord Colonsay; access is either straight up the hill behind the harbour or by an old track starting from the church across the road from the hotel in Scalasaig. This is an easy walk, accessible even by an electric wheelchair, and it provides a fine view of the harbour and of the island of Jura to the south-east.

The village of Scalasaig is a scatter of houses around the harbour and hotel. There is a petrol station and one shop, which also includes a post office. The name comes from the Norse language: 'shell bay', or 'Skallj's bay' – 'Skalli', meaning 'bald-headed', was a common Viking nickname, and occurs in place-names throughout Argyll.

The hotel complex now includes three self-catering units, ideal for family holidays. The hotel itself has eleven bedrooms, most with private bathrooms. The public bar is the pivot of Colonsay's information network, and is much appreciated by locals and visitors. Here titled aristocracy and lobster fishermen rub shoulders with holidaymakers. Good quality bar food is available. The hotel restaurant is a gastronomic delight; good food, beautifully cooked and presented, and a good range of wines. Mention must be made both of the desserts, designed to promote long walks the next day as a necessary corrective, and of the Sunday dinner menu which includes locally grown oysters. The bedrooms are warm, centrally heated, comfortable, and well furnished. As mentioned above, bicycles are available free to hotel guests. A courtesy car from the hotel meets ferries, on request.

The road system of Colonsay consists of an eight-mile circular loop around the middle of the island, with spurs to the north and south – fourteen miles in all. Proceeding clockwise, there is a road junction just half a mile west of the hotel; this is the turnoff for the south end of Colonsay, and for Oronsay. Continuing round the loop, the first farm reached is Machrins (Gaelic: 'machairean', 'coastal pastures'). Here a track leads off to the south, crossing the 18-hole golf course and a grass airstrip, eventually reaching Ardskenish (G.: 'ard', 'point' + Norse: 'skeinish', 'war-galley point'). Past Machrins the road reaches the western coast at Port Mor (G.: 'the big port'), then turns inland again at the ruined medieval chapel of Kilchattan (G.: 'the church of Cattan', an early Christian Irish saint). Nearby are the standing stones known as 'Fingal's Limpet Hammers', after the great hero of Irish folklore. The road runs eastwards along Loch Fada (G.: 'the long loch'), now divided into three separate parts due to improved drainage and reclamation. Passing the old mill, the road reaches the entrance to Colonsay House, then turns sharply to the south. At this point a spur leads north to Uragaig, Kiloran Bay and Balnahard. The circular loop passes Kiloran Hall, crosses Loch Fada on reclaimed land, and returns to Scalasaig by way of a hairpin bend at Turraman Loch.

The southern spur off this loop leads past Milbuie (G.:

'yellow hill') to Garvard (G.: 'rough point'), passing the road ends leading to Balerumindubh and Baleruminmore (G.: 'the dark marsh farm' and 'the big marsh farm'). This last track is well trodden by MacPhees, for the last chieftain of their clan was killed against a stone cross in an old burial ground near Baleruminmore farmhouse. The main road reaches the south coast of Colonsay, and it is here, at low tide, that a track crosses the sandy tidal flats known as 'the Strand', passing the Hangman's Rock, to reach the island of Oronsay, where a mile of farm track leads past the prehistoric fort of Dùn Domhnuill (G.: 'Donald's Fort') to the priory and farmhouse. On the south-eastern coast of the island are shell mounds dating from the fifth millennium BC, evidence of the existence of coastal communities of hunter-gatherers. A small airstrip occupies the centre of the island.

The times when Oronsay can be reached safely are posted in the hotel lobby in Scalasaig. As a general rule, the Strand is dry for between two to four hours at each low tide, but conditions can change quickly according to the changeable and somewhat unpredictable weather. In some circumstances the tide will not go out at all. Try not to take a car over to Oronsay. The locals would never dream of driving over, unless in an old banger near the end of its life, because of corrosion caused by the salt water. Exercise caution: a stalled car will be covered with seven feet of water at high tide whereas stranded pedestrians will suffer the inconvenience of waiting for the next low tide. When in doubt, visitors should always follow local advice, and not take any chances.

The name 'Oronsay' has proved puzzling to scholars, and it is not possible to be too dogmatic about its meaning. Some would like to see a connection with the Irish saint Oran (Odhran), and for this reason the spelling 'Oransay' is popular locally, meaning 'Oran's island'. But the local pronunciation 'Orasa', without an 'n' and with the accent on the first syllable, suggests another explanation. It may derive from the Norse 'orfiris-ey', 'ebb-tide island' meaning an island which is only an island at high water. There are

14

also four Oronsays in the Outer Hebrides and two in Skye which fit this explanation exactly.

Scholars also find it difficult to agree about Colonsay's name. Again, the 'n' is not sounded in Gaelic, making it unlikely that it has anything to do with St Columba (Colum). Constantly confused with the nearby island of Coll in early records, it seems more likely that the name comes, not from an individual by the name of Colla (possibly remembered in Dùn Cholla), but from the Norse 'koll-r', a hill-top, + 'ey', island).

Returning to Colonsay House, there is a further two miles of roadway to the farms of Uragaig (N.: 'ox bay') and Duntealtaig (G.: 'dùn ceilte', 'the hidden fort'), passing the south end of Kiloran Bay. A farm track turns off to the north, leading to Balnahard (G.: 'baile na h-àirde', 'the farm on the point'), and eventually to Balnahard Bay, but this track is *not* passable for ordinary motor vehicles, without serious consequences to exhaust systems and gearboxes.

It does, however, make for one of the most interesting walks on Colonsay. The sands of Kiloran Bay are backed by an extensive sand dune system, in which Viking burials have been found. The Balnahard track then ascends the shoulder of Colonsay's highest hill, Carnan Eoin (G.: 'cairn (or rocky heap) of the birds'). It is an easy scramble from the track to the summit at a height of 143m (470ft), from where there are extensive views. You are likely to see wild goats on the slopes of Carnan Eoin, and perhaps an eagle. Further up the track is Tobar Challuim Chille, 'St Columba's Well', while past the farm of Balnahard is a medieval chapel and burial ground, with a stone cross. Geologists will regard a visit to Balnahard Bay as essential, because of the outcrops of gneiss there, while they will find the natural arches and igneous dykes of Kiloran Bay equally interesting.

The cliffs beyond Uragaig are worth visiting for their sea birds, as well as for a couple of ancient forts, but as they are extremely steep and slippery, caution is advised, especially in wet and windy conditions. There are no roads or tracks on the west side of Colonsay, north of Kilchattan, or on the east side, north of Riasg Buidhe, but there is much of interest in these areas for the naturalist and archaeologist, and the walking is not too difficult.

This whirlwind tour of Colonsay and Oronsay is intended to aid the visitor, or armchair traveller, in grasping the main features of the islands. Detailed discussion of many of the places and historical sites referred to above will be found in later chapters. However, the purpose of this book is not to provide the reader with an encyclopedic knowledge of the islands, but to demonstrate something of the range of interest and fascination which make Colonsay and Oronsay an increasingly popular destination. Readers seeking further information will find suggestions for further reading in a bibliography at the end of this volume. The works by Symington Grieve (1923) and John de Vere Loder (1935), both regrettably out of print, are particularly recommended.

2 GEOLOGY AND LANDSCAPE

The landscape and scenery we admire today on the islands of Colonsay and Oronsay are the result of millions of years of erosion and geological changes, from 2,500-million-year-old Lewisian gneiss to raised beaches and sand dunes created within the last 10,000 years. The appearance of the islands has changed many times throughout the geological eons and, even within the period of human settlement, changes in sea level have drastically altered the coastline several times.

TORRIDONIAN

Most of Colonsay and Oronsay is made up of sedimentary rocks originally deposited as layers of mud and sand on the sea bed and eventually transformed by pressure and the passage of time into rocks, such as mudstones and sandstones. Over millions of years these sediments were buried to a depth of several miles, where they underwent stresses and strains deep down in the earth and became deformed and folded, so that the original horizontal strata became almost unrecognisable. Eventually all these rocks were uplifted by pressure from below, and thousands of feet of overlying material were eroded by time and glaciations, leaving the varied exposures we see today.

Most geologists regard these sedimentary rocks as belonging to the Torridonian era, dating back about 900 million years, but it is difficult to be sure. There are no fossils in any of these rocks, and it is not practicable to apply radiometric dating techniques, so there is room for argument amongst academic geologists, some of whom would place Colonsay's rocks as 'recent' as only 600 million years old, dating them to the Dalradian period – also found on the island of Islay to the south. The most recent geological research (Bentley, Maltman and Fitches, 1988) discusses the possibility of Colonsay and parts of Islay being 'a suspect terrane within the Scottish Caledonides'. The authors claim that because the rocks of Colonsay and Islay are 'difficult to correlate with rocks in adjacent areas', it is best to regard them as 'stratigraphically unique'; they 'probably originated at some distance and were transported to their present location'. A displacement of between 100 and 200km (60 to 120 miles) is considered likely. Details of this radical geological article can be found in the bibliography.

Whatever their absolute age, it is possible to build up a relative chronology, based on the relationship of one type of sedimentary rock to another. This shows the following succession: 1, Oronsay group (sandstones below, mudstones above); 2, Dùn Gallain group (epidotic grits); 3, Machrins group (grits and mudstones); 4, Kilchattan group (phyllites and sandstones); 5, Milbuie group (epidotic grits and phyllites); 6, Kiloran flag group (very uniform and constant); 7, Colonsay limestone group; 8, Staosnaig phyllite group.

While it may take training as a geologist or mineralogist to distinguish between these eight groups of sedimentary rocks, all of which exhibit marked differences within each group according to local circumstances, for example in colour and grain-size, these variations make it easy for even the casual observer to see the bedded, sedimentary nature of the deposits. Looking across Kiloran Bay to the slopes of Carnan Eoin, the angled beds of sandstones and limestone can be clearly seen.

The rocks of Colonsay and Oronsay have had an important influence on the way human settlement developed, and on the economic prosperity of the islands, both in the past and now. W. H. Murray, in his book *The Hebrides* (1966), says that 'Colonsay was born with a silver spoon in her mouth'. He is referring not to a precious metal, but to limestone, which has given fertility and prosperity to agriculturists over the

18

centuries. Outcrops can be seen around Kiloran Bay, around Scalasaig, and around Balerumindubh. Areas of Colonsay and Oronsay covered by marine sands and gravels, for example raised beach deposits, are also extremely fertile.

LEWISIAN GNEISS

In one small part of Colonsay it is possible to glimpse the 'basement' rock on which all the sedimentary rocks were deposited. On the north side of Balnahard Bay, at the far north of the island, the ancient metamorphic rock known as gneiss (pronounced 'nice') is found. Gneiss is a crystalline rock, consisting of quartz, hornblende, feldspar and mica, sometimes almost resembling granite. This rock, although metamorphosed from its original form by great heat and pressure, is the oldest rock in Europe, and is known as Lewisian gneiss after the island of Lewis in the Outer Hebrides. All of that long chain of islands is composed of gneiss, and it also occurs on the mainland of north-west Scotland, on the Sleat peninsula of Skye, in Coll and Tiree, and in the Rinns of Islay. Colonsay gneiss is a coarse-grained banded quartzo-feldspar rock with dark knots and streaks.

It is humbling to handle something so old. The gneiss of the Outer Isles is reckoned to be more than half the age of the Earth, at 2,500,000,000 years; on Colonsay it is likely to be only 'slightly' younger, at 2,000 million years – quite a conversation piece back home in suburbia for the urban refugees who visit Colonsay every year!

Adjoining the gneiss, on the slope of Leac Bhuidhe, can be seen an example of a type of rock known as a conglomerate. This was originally sand full of pebbles, which was the first sediment to be deposited on the gneiss after it was exposed to the Earth's surface about 1,500 million years ago.

IGNEOUS INTRUSIONS

Among the more obvious geological features of Colonsay are igneous rocks, intruding into the Torridonian beds at

19

several points. These represent solidified magma, the most recent of which were forced to the surface through cracks in the Earth's crust about 60 million years ago. The igneous intrusions at the north end of Kiloran Bay, lying just above the low water mark, are amongst the clearest examples anywhere of this phenomenon. The dyke runs along the length of the beach, emerging from the sand about half way along, at the east edge of an outcrop of folded phyllites, a mica-rich rock that glistens in the sun. The softer rocks have been weathered away, leaving the dyke standing proud for about 65ft (20m). It is a lamprophyre dyke (from the Greek meaning 'bright porphyry'), and consists of a medium-grained igneous rock. Farther along the beach the dyke crosses another outcrop, this time a volcanic breccia – a rock made up of cemented angular fragments, usually resulting from a volcanic explosion. Because of constant sandblasting and polishing by sand and sea water the structure of the breccia shows up exceptionally clearly. On the north side of this outcrop, just above low water mark, can be seen another intrusion, of syenite, a coarse-grained igneous rock, often pinkish in colour because it is rich in feldspar. This is a far older intrusion than the lamprophyre dyke, being about 400 million years old. It gets its name from Syene, in Egypt. Black spots of hornblende also occur in this syenite.

Another, larger intrusion of syenite appears as a low reef on the seaward side of the breccia outcrop. The dyke disappears under the sand once more, but can be seen again at the north end of the bay, climbing up through more phyllites. One begins to get some idea of the three-dimensional character of Tertiary dykes, which so often appear only as narrow stripes on the country rock, but of course may have a vertical depth of thousands of feet.

Another area on Colonsay where a rather spectacular igneous intrusion can be seen is around Scalasaig, where a mass of diorite occupies the lower ground, intruding into the surrounding Torridonian sandstones, limestone and slate.

Diorite is a coarse-grained igneous rock with clearly defined crystals of feldspar, mica, hornblende and augite. Contact with the Torridonian rocks can be seen on the slopes of the hill under Lord Colonsay's monument, and also to the north of the hotel, where another breccia can be seen at the boundary of the intrusion. The low, wooded ridge running westwards from Scalasaig pier, parallel to the road, is composed of diorite.

There are many igneous dykes around the coast. At Port Mor, where the coast road turns inland, there is a basalt dyke on the south side of the cove. Just before the end of the road to the Strand a basalt dyke is to the east of the road. This dyke is about 2m (6½ft) wide; the dark olive-green rock is weathered to a dark reddish-brown colour. Other easily accessible dykes can be seen on the shore to the north of the pier at Scalasaig.

On the western horizon, the lighthouse of Dubh Artach is built on an igneous intrusion of basalt which rises just above sea level.

FAULTS

On a slightly larger scale, one of the most obvious geological features on Colonsay is the fault line occupied by Loch Fada, which almost splits the island in two – and indeed, at one time, did so. Another fault is revealed by the valley followed by the road west of Scalasaig, running across to the west coast of the island. A much larger fault lies under the sea about 5km (3 miles) to the west of Colonsay – the Great Glen fault, which almost bisects Scotland between Inverness and Fort William, and can be traced along the line of Loch Linnhe and the Firth of Lorn, running south-west out into the Atlantic. Another large fault lies to the east of Colonsay, running into Islay as the Loch Skerrols Thrust. The horizontal displacement produced by these two large offshore faults may account for the general disparity of the rock outcrops of Islay, Colonsay and Oronsay compared to the surrounding areas.

GLACIATION

The gneiss at Balnahard would have once been buried to a depth of more than 20km (12 miles), giving some idea of the effect of erosion and glaciation on this part of Scotland. At several places on Colonsay and Oronsay, the distinctive striations ('striae') or scratches left by the ice-sheets that have passed over the islands several times in the last 2 million years can be seen. The last Ice Age ended about 20000BC, and has left its mark on the landscape. The eastern coast of Colonsay owes its rather boring, eroded appearance to ice action, there are areas of glacial moraine in the faulted valleys around Loch Fada and Scalasaig, and there are several examples of a glacial landform known as *roches moutonnées*, because rocks have been left like a recumbent sheep's back. One of the finest examples is on Oronsay – the rocky scarp crowned by the Iron Age fort of Dùn Domhnuill (NR354890). Another fort, Dùn Gallain (NR348931), is on a prominent ice-rounded hill west of Machrins. Examples of striations can be seen along the track leading from Glassard to Riasg Buidhe.

Another effect of glaciation can be seen on any of Colonsay's beaches, but especially on the west coast. Here will be found a great variety of rocks alien to the islands, brought by ice from the east. Granite from the north end of Loch Fyne, mica porphyry from around Inveraray and Furnace, old red sandstone, Lorn lavas, quartzites from Jura, even flint pebbles from Mull or even possibly from Aberdeenshire; there are many exotic specimens available for the eagle-eyed rockhound. A good hunting ground is the pebble beach (NR357943) to the south-west of Port Mor, near Lower Kilchattan. There is a large boulder of Loch Fyne granite below the car park at the south end of Kiloran Bay.

RAISED BEACHES

Looking back towards Uragaig from the north end of Kiloran Bay, the cliff and rock platform of what was once a beach but is now 135ft (41m) above sea level can be seen. On the island of Oronsay, at the same height, an ancient beach, backed by high cliffs, occupies the ground between Oronsay Priory and the summit of Beinn Oronsay. The flat ground between Balerumindubh and Baleruminmore, again now far above current sea level, was once washed by the sea.

There have been many changes in sea level over geological time, and it was not until about 5000BC that the coastline became more or less what it is today. The detail of these changes is complex, and best left to academic specialists, but in general terms what happened is easily understood. As the ice-sheets melted, starting from about 20000BC, sea levels rose fairly quickly as vast amounts of water were released into the world's oceans. However, this process was counter-acted by the fact that with the great weight of ice no longer pressing it down, the land began to rise – a process known as isostatic recovery. This recovery was much slower than the melting of the ice, and it took about 15,000 years for a situation of stability and equilibrium to develop. The ice may have been 1,600m (5,000ft) thick over the central spine of Scotland; over Colonsay it was perhaps 600m (2,000ft) thick at its maximum extent. Along the coastlines nearest to Rannoch Moor, where the ice was thickest and heaviest, isostatic recovery was greatest. But farther away, where the ice-sheet was thinner and isostatic recovery correspondingly less, the increase in sea level exceeded the rise of the land, and pre-glacial coastlines were flooded. This can be seen in Orkney and Shetland. On the western coastline of the Outer Hebrides some Iron Age duns dating from around 200BC to AD200 are now largely under water and the land there is still being gradually submerged.

SAND

Most of Oronsay consists of blown sand and dunes, and there are extensive areas of sand on Colonsay, at Balnahard,

Kiloran Bay, Machrins, and Ardskenish, with odd pockets elsewhere. The dunes at Balnahard are now a Site of Special Scientific Interest (SSSI). Under a management agreement between the Nature Conservancy Council and the local farmer these dunes have been fenced off and are grazed only in winter, allowing a spectacular proliferation of plant growth. It is difficult to know how old some of the dune systems might be, as it is known that they can advance (or retreat) quite rapidly. The Kiloran dunes are impressive, adding yet another feature to an already amazing natural environment. These desert landscapes are a delight for small children, rabbits, and botanists, and are welcomed by picknickers for the shelter they provide from the wind, and by archaeologists for their preservation of ancient burials.

PEAT

The most recent 'geological' deposition on Colonsay took place well after human settlement was established. The peat deposits, which cover the poorly drained parts of the island, formed after about 1200BC when the climate deteriorated quite suddenly. Archaeological fieldwork on Beinn Arnicil has revealed the remains of an extensive agricultural field-system, complete with field dykes, stock enclosures, and house sites, all likely to have been used in the Bronze Age, and abandoned when poor weather made upland cultivation no longer worthwhile.

MINERAL RESOURCES

No minerals or precious metals occur in large enough quantities to be economically feasible. The only possible economic use of any of Colonsay's rocks and minerals would appear to be imaginative small-scale marketing of polished beach pebbles, or of Balnahard gneiss – perhaps tourists could be persuaded to buy an attractively presented specimen of 'the oldest rocks in Europe'.

CLIMATE

It will come as no surprise to either residents or visitors to the West of Scotland to learn that in the past, as today, the weather has dominated island life. There is, of course, a difference between weather and climate; whereas meteorologists try to predict whether or not it will rain tomorrow, climatologists deal in long term trends and averages.

Around 5000BC their primitive predecessors would have noticed a marked improvement in average temperatures, as a sudden and dramatic change in the climate caused temperatures to rise throughout Europe to an average of 2°C (3.6F) above today's levels. The climate became warmer, and wetter; the extra rain encouraged forest growth, and the whole of Colonsay and Oronsay would have been covered by trees and scrub. Birch and hazel spread to their maximum extent, and willow did well in the favourable conditions. But the heavy rain leached the thin island soils, while the growth of sphagnum moss and accumulating peat on higher ground robbed scrub hazel and birch of soil for regeneration, and the tree line retreated again. At the end of this climatic period, known as the Atlantic period, the first Neolithic farmers came to Scotland's Atlantic islands.

Between 3000BC and 2000BC the climate became much drier, though the higher average temperatures continued. This period is known as the sub-Boreal, and represents the climatic optimum in north-west Europe. By around 1200BC the dry and sunny climate of the sub-Boreal period had come to an end, and a cold and wet climate developed during the sub-Atlantic period. Without human interference, the forest which covered all of Colonsay and the neighbouring islands would have continued to the present day. The bare aspect of most of the Hebrides is due entirely to the interventions of mankind, from the forest clearance of Neolithic and Bronze

Age farmers to the overgrazing caused by the introduction of sheep.

The sub-Atlantic climate is basically the one we endure today, although over the last three thousand years there have been some climatic ups and downs. There was a period of milder climate from AD1000 to 1200, sometimes offered as a determinist explanation for Viking expansion. Certainly improved climatic conditions, with an average temperature rise of 2 to 4°C (4 to 7°F), made their long sea voyages to the Hebrides, Iceland, Greenland and North America marginally less dangerous.

Perhaps, too, a slight deterioration between AD1550 and AD1700, when the climate turned colder and glaciers in the Alps and in Scandinavia advanced for the first time since the end of the last Ice Age, had a destabilising effect on an already fragile Hebridean economy.

The climate in Colonsay today could be described as mild, wet and windy. Basic records of temperature and rainfall have been kept at a weather station at Kiloran for the last fifty years. These give a picture of relatively cool summers and surprisingly mild winters. The warmest months of the year are July and August, with averages of around 13.7°C (56.7°F), while the coldest months are January and February, with averages of 4.5°C (40.1°F), giving an annual range of temperature of about 9°C (14.5°F) compared with between 12 and 13°C (21 and 23°F) for many inland and eastern areas of Britain. The mildness of the winters is particularly striking. From 1963 to 1980, records from Colonsay show that air temperatures dropped below freezing point for an average of only 21 days in the year.

Rainfall figures for Colonsay are surprisingly low, compared with other parts of western Scotland. Average annual rainfall for Colonsay is about 1,300mm (50in) and may well drop to 1,100mm (46in) for the more low-lying areas in the south and east of Oronsay. This compares with 1,500mm (58in) on the coasts of Islay and Jura, 1,800mm (70in) on the mainland coast near Oban, and 3,000mm (117in) or more in the mountainous interior of the Highlands. Seasonal variation is quite marked. The driest months are from March to June. The figures increase gradually throughout the summer months and reach a peak from September to January. The rainfall in Colonsay for the months of October and December is likely to be double that for April and May.

James Wilson, on a tour of inspection for the Fishery Commissioners in June 1841, described meteorological conditions on the hill road from Scalasaig to Kiloran: 'The rain drove against us all the way like split peas . . .the road had by this time been converted in many places to something like a muddy river . . . It is a sustaining thought to know that one is serving Queen and country.' Of such moral fibre was the British Empire built!

Snow is almost unknown. Records kept at Rhuvaal lighthouse only 10km (6 miles) to the south-east of Oronsay suggest that although detectable snowfall may occur on 10 to 20 days in the year, it only lies on the ground for an average of 1.2 days.

Measurable amounts of rain fall on at least half the days in the year, but there is a surprising amount of fine, sunny weather. Sunshine records are not available for Colonsay, but records kept in Tiree, 60km (36miles) to the north-west, suggest that this is the sunniest area in Scotland, with annual averages of 1,300 hours a year – around 4 hours of sunshine per day, which compares very well with many parts of southern England. Again, there is pronounced seasonal variation, with the best of the sunshine being in May and June. On average one can expect two hours of sunshine a day in winter and six hours or more in summer. On a fine summer's day, eighteen hours of sunshine are possible!

From a human point of view, the dominating feature of the weather is the wind, which most of the time varies from strong to unrelenting. The exceptions are cherished and appreciated all the more. No data are available for Colonsay, but Tiree records show marked seasonal variations in both wind intensity and direction. Gales are rare from May to August, but occur on between 3 and 5 days a month in October and November, increasing to 7 to 8 days a month in December and January – roughly one day in four. Strong winds can blow from almost any direction at any time of the year, but from January to March most of the winds tend to be from the south or south-east, while from September to November they tend to come from the south-west, west, and north-west.

Weather reports from Tiree will give an idea of what to expect on Colonsay and Oronsay – Tiree is the nearest 'coastal station' and comes right at the beginning of the shipping forecasts broadcast on radio. The relevant 'sea areas' are Malin and Hebrides.

As you stand on the western shore of Colonsay and look out over a distant seascape and a boundless sky, it is impossible not to be aware of the constant ebb and flow of weather. Colonsay and Oronsay and the rest of the British Isles are on a meteorological battleground, upon which streams of continental and oceanic air advance and retreat endlessly. If the airstream is easterly, the dry continental air can bring long periods of heat and sunshine to the West Highlands in summer, and long, crispy clear periods of sunshine in the winter. The prevailing westerly airstreams are moister, and more likely to bring rain. The processes involved are described graphically and in detail by Frank Fraser Darling and John Morton Boyd in *The Highlands and Islands*.

Visitors will always hope for good weather, but in our sub-Atlantic climate there are no guarantees, only wishful thinking, and in the absence of a direct line to the Almighty certain precautions are essential. Adequate raingear and correct footwear will make it possible to have a good time, whatever the weather. Inadequate protection leads inevitably to saturation, cold, misery, recriminations and regret. Wet clothing can be dried out – eventually – but without doubt prevention is the best cure. Even on a fine day there is likely to be a brisk breeze, and light, windproof jackets or anoraks should always be carried. The weather can change quickly, and although inadequately clad walkers are unlikely to come to any harm in these gentle landscapes, they can certainly become exceedingly miserable very quickly.

Correct footwear is most important. Proper walking boots, with Vibram soles, are best, and need not be expensive or heavy. Good walking shoes are acceptable only for farm tracks or beachcombing expeditions. Trainers will become soaked in anything but drought conditions and can be ruined quickly and easily. Wellies are uncomfortable to walk in for any distance and are positively dangerous in wet conditions, but they are useful for crossing the Strand to Oronsay. If you buy new boots or shoes for your island adventure, don't forget to come well-provided with plasters to deal with the inevitable blisters!

In this chapter it has been possible to provide only a summary of the main features of the geology, climate and landscape of Colonsay and Oronsay, but more detailed information can be obtained from the books and maps referred to. After this introduction to the physical environment, it is natural to proceed to examine the flora and fauna of the islands, starting with the post-glacial colonisation of plants and animals.

3 PLANTS AND ANIMALS

The natural environment of the Inner Hebrides has been studied extensively in recent years, and our appreciation of the 'green' issues affecting them has even reached the pages of tabloid newspapers, which eagerly took up the controversy involving peat, whisky, farmers, conservation, and Greenland white-fronted geese on the island of Islay.

As far as Colonsay and Oronsay are concerned, some of the most interesting work on the natural history of the islands arose from the archaeological excavations of shell mounds on Oronsay under the direction of Paul Mellars. His teams of specialists studied the past and present natural environment in great detail and the importance of their contribution is gratefully acknowledged.

At the moment, natural history records for Colonsay and Oronsay are being collected and collated by John and Pamela Clarke of Milbuie, who are happy to provide information and assistance to interested visitors. They can provide species lists for local flora and fauna and they occasionally give lectures on natural history. A great deal of detailed study remains to be done, but we now have a good understanding of the range of species present. Anything unusual found by visitors should be treated with respect, and reported.

MAMMALS

Compared to the larger islands of Islay and Jura, Colonsay and Oronsay have a much smaller range of mammalian species, suggesting that at least since the end of the last Ice Age, the islands have been isolated. In the Mesolithic middens of Oronsay, bones of the red deer (*Cervus elaphus*), pig (*Sus scrofa*), grey seal (*Halichoerus grypus*), porpoise (*Phocaena phocaena*), dolphin (*Delphinus delphis*), and otter (*Lutra lutra*) have all been positively identified, often in large numbers. Analysis of these bones suggested seasonal exploitation of red deer and grey seals.

There are no deer on the islands today, but two breeding colonies of the Atlantic grey seal (*Halichoerus grypus*) are centred on the small islands of Eilean nan Ron (G.: 'seal island') and Eilean Ghaoideamal, lying off the south and east coasts of Oronsay. The total adult population of both colonies in 1956 was 269, with 350 to 400 pups born in a season. In 1981 305 grey seal pups were counted on Eilean nan Ron and 440 on the other Oronsay skerries, out of a total number of 1,940 pups for the whole of the Inner Hebrides, including Nave Island, Gunna and the Treshnish Islands. It was thought that the total population of grey seals in the Inner Hebrides was around 8,000.

Grey seals can often be seen lying on the skerries between Colonsay and Oronsay, and particularly on the rock platforms around Eilean nan Ron, at low tide. The Atlantic grey seal is one of the world's rarest mammals, with a total world population of around 50,000, of which perhaps half breed around the western coasts of Scotland. A few common seals (*Phoca vitulina*) can usually be seen in the same area, although the two species will not mix, even when sharing the same rock. Adults can easily be distinguished by their appearance and behaviour. Grey seals are much larger than common seals – an adult male can be up to 3.8m (12ft) long and can weigh up to 320kg (700lb). Adult male common seals reach a maximum length of 2m (6ft) and can weigh 100kg (220lb). It is not so easy to identify juveniles – young grey seals, at a distance, look very much like adult common seals. The common seal has a much shorter face than the grey seal, and when disturbed, almost seems to turn up its nose as it looks at you, unlike the grey seal, which has a distinctly 'Roman-nosed' appearance.

According to Pennant (1772), 'the seals are here numerous: a few are caught in nets placed between the rocks'. At one time nets were placed in the narrow tidal rivers left by the tide between Colonsay and Oronsay. It is thought that seals were hunted for their oil.

Alfred Erskine Gathorne-Hardy, writing in 1914, gives long descriptions of seal-hunting and seal behaviour based on shooting expeditions on Colonsay and Oronsay by himself and his second son, Alfred Cecil Gathorne-Hardy. The two of them managed to supply a specimen to the Natural History Museum on Cromwell Road in London within 36 hours of it being shot near Ardskenish. It was put on display and was a feature of interest in the museum for many years.

During the viral epidemic, which decimated North Sea seal populations in 1988–89, seal colonies off the west coast of Scotland were monitored closely. While many deaths did occur, and many carcasses were washed up on local beaches, it was clear that the epidemic was nothing like as widespread and devastating as had been feared. Only further monitoring and seal counts in the years to come will reveal the true extent of the effects of the epidemic, but at present it looks as though the seal populations will not be permanently affected. In any case, it is difficult to see what could be done to help; sadly this appears to be one of those circumstances where Nature has to be left to sort things out, since human intervention is likely to cause more harm than good. However, scientific research may be able to establish the cause of the epidemic, and any human culpability, and take remedial action.

Other marine mammals are seen only occasionally. Rorquals (*Balaenoptera physalus*) are sometimes seen, while a 24-metre-long (78¾ft) blue whale (*Balaenoptera musculus*) was stranded near Balnahard on the northern coast of Colonsay in July 1916. Minke whale are seen regularly.

Of the smaller land animals, pygmy shrews (*Sorex minutus*), house mice (*Mus musculus*) now possibly extinct, field mice

(*Apodemus sylvaticus*), and brown rats (*Rattus norvegicus*) have all been recorded, of which only the first is likely to be native, the others all having been introduced. It is thought that rabbits (*Oryctolagus cuniculus*) were introduced from the island of Barra in the eighteenth century, when a warren was dug for them at Kiloran. The common hare (*Lepus capensis*) seems to have been in the islands at one time, probably introduced for sport, but has died out. There are small herds of wild goats on Oronsay and in two areas of Colonsay. They can often be seen from the track leading from Kiloran to Balnahard. Strictly speaking they are 'feral', meaning they are descended from formerly domestic stock. Local tradition states that they may be descended from goats shipwrecked in 1588, from the remnants of the Spanish Armada. It is known that goats were carried on board some of the ships.

The pipistrelle bat (*Pipistrellus pipistrellus*) became common in the islands in the late nineteenth century. The long-eared bat (*Plecotus auritus*) is also present. Both have been recorded using a 'bat detector', an electronic contraption which converts the distinctive 'radar' emissions of each bat species into audible sound.

The otter (*Lutra lutra*) is the only carnivore on the islands, and is common around the southern coasts of Colonsay, especially along the Strand between Colonsay and Oronsay. It is a playful animal, and has a habit of feeding while floating on its back. It is, however, elusive; the best time to see otters is early in the morning or late on a summer evening, when they can often be spotted close inshore. They will eat a wide range of sea and freshwater fish, as well as crustaceans, birds and small mammals.

Place-names suggest that two other animals, now absent, once lived on the islands. The polecat, now extinct in Scotland, was said to be plentiful in 1549; there is a place on Oronsay called Lag nam Feòcullan ('polecat hollow'). The pine marten (*Martes martes*) is referred to in several place-names in Colonsay, such as at Lèana an Taghain ('pine

33

marten meadow') at Baleruminmore, providing evidence of greater tree cover in the past.

The relative impoverishment of vertebrate fauna on Colonsay and Oronsay is probably due to the fact that the islands have been geographically separated from the Scottish mainland for so long. The neighbouring islands of Islay and Jura have a wider range of species, but it is known that they were connected to the mainland by a land bridge well into postglacial times. Eleven species recorded from Islay and Jura are not present on Colonsay and Oronsay, including the Arctic hare, stoat, roe deer, red deer, common frog, common toad, and adder. Several species absent from Islay and Jura, notably the hedgehog, red squirrel, water vole, fox, weasel, wild cat and badger, were all part of the early postglacial fauna of Britain, and these are also 'missing' from Colonsay and Oronsay. Records are somewhat haphazard, and the lists produced by Loder in 1935 probably need amending. Further research on the natural history of Colonsay and Oronsay will undoubtedly add to our understanding of these questions.

BIRDS

A species list for the islands, with discussion and references to published sources, has been compiled by Jardine, Clarke and Clarke (1986). The Clarkes, who live at Milbuie, have the advantage over all previous writers (except for D. R. Alexander who produced a list privately in 1979) of being residents, rather than occasional visitors or passing migrants. Their 60-page booklet is essential for all serious ornithologists visiting Colonsay and Oronsay. They reckon that it is possible for the average birdwatcher to see at least fifty species in a day without ever leaving the road, and claim that 'a more experienced watcher could well be rewarded with seventy or even eighty species'. They give records for 214 species, from wrens to golden eagles, though many of these are for only one or two sightings.

The wide range of habitats in the islands accounts for

the diverse range of species observable. The numerous small freshwater lochs provide a feeding, breeding and roosting environment for many species, including little grebe, mallard, teal, pochard, goldeneye, greylag goose, red-throated diver, cormorant, heron, reed bunting and sedge warbler. Coastal skerries, with their high tidal range, are good feeding grounds for turnstone, oystercatcher, curlew, purple sandpiper and heron, while coastal shallows provide a perfect habitat for feeding auks, duck, sawbills and divers. Sandy beaches provide good foraging for ringed plover, dunlin, oystercatcher, purple sandpiper and sanderling, while the rotting seaweed at high water mark is attractive to species such as linnet, twite, rock pipit, meadow pipit, pied wagtail, song thrush, chough and dunnock. The dunes behind the beach at Kiloran and elsewhere are a good feeding habitat for chough, ringed plover, oystercatcher, lapwing, golden plover and curlew, and a nesting area for skylark, shelduck and wheatear. At the Strand, it is quite possible to see fifteen species of birds from a parked car, if the tide is coming in.

Inland cliffs provide nest sites for buzzard, hooded crow, starling and jackdaw, while the western sea cliffs have large seabird colonies: fulmar, kittiwake, raven, hooded crow ('hoodies'), jackdaw, starling, rock pipit, four other species of gull and three species of auk. Around the hotel at Scalasaig, and in the woods around Colonsay House, all the common garden and woodland birds can be seen. From the vantage point at Loch Turraman there are regular sightings of pheasant, sparrowhawk, tufted duck, heron, mallard, teal, goldeneye, greylag goose, whooper swan, buzzard and occasionally other birds of prey.

In the fields around Kiloran farm, white-fronted geese, barnacle geese, Canada geese and curlew can be seen in good numbers from October to early May. Latest figures (1988) suggest a winter population of about 250 barnacles, 120 white-fronts, 55 greylags, and 50 Canada geese. The Canada geese, and a few greylags, breed on Colonsay. Canada geese were introduced in 1934 by Lord Strathcona's gamekeeper, supposedly in an attempt to improve the number of wintering wildfowl. It was hoped that their loud calls would attract migrating geese and persuade them to land and take up winter residence in Colonsay. Although migrant goose populations *did* increase in numbers thereafter, this was probably due to other factors, as the Canada goose is larger and more aggressive than other species and, if anything, its presence would tend to discourage them from landing. A more plausible reason for the introduction of Canada geese was perhaps simply to provide a breeding population for sporting purposes. Bird experts argue over these matters, and as goose counts over the years have given rather inconsistent results, it is necessary to be cautious. Probably the counts made from aircraft should be preferred, compared to the higher figures provided by Kiloran gamekeepers.

The chough, which is one of Britain's rarest breeding birds, has made something of a comeback in recent years. Once common, it declined during the nineteenth century and was no longer breeding in Colonsay by about 1914. At the turn of the century the chough was 'an everyday sight' at the north end of the island. A farmer told Gathorne-Hardy that when he was a boy choughs were numerous and commonly eaten; he thought the increase of jackdaws had supplanted the choughs' breeding sites and had contributed to the diminution in their numbers. A few pairs now nest on Colonsay, and small flocks can often be seen feeding in the dunes at Kiloran. By contrast, the corncrake population is declining, as it is in other parts of Britain. Changes in farming practice, especially the preference for silage over hay, and other agricultural improvements, have deprived this secretive bird of much of its habitat. It has been suggested that the modern tendency towards lambing on enclosed pasture rather than on the hill ground, taking a grass crop later in the year, is also a factor. The corncrake's distinctive call can still sometimes be heard on the islands – something like a grated comb, or the rattle that used to be common at football matches.

The shell mounds on Oronsay have yielded bird bones:

red-breasted merganser, shelduck, shag, cormorant, gannet, ringed plover, guillemot, razorbill, and unidentified species of gull and tern were all eaten by the Mesolithic hunter/gatherers. But it was the discovery of bones of the now extinct great auk (*Alca impennis*) which excited naturalist Symington Grieve in the 1880s, and resulted in a book, *The Great Auk, or Garefowl: its history, archaeology, and remains* (1885).

Symington Grieve first visited Oronsay in 1879, the beginning of a long association with the islands which was to result in the publication of two books and many shorter articles on history, archaeology, natural history and folklore. At first he was interested only in making a list of the island's flora, but in May 1880 he noticed the mound which he says was known to the islanders as Caisteal-nan-Gillean. He gives the Gaelic meaning as 'the castle of the servants' (gillies or followers), though the more usual derivation is 'Maclean's castle'.

In 1881 he met William Galloway, a noted antiquarian who had interested himself over many years in the ancient ruins and sculptured stones of Scotland. It was arranged that they would visit Oronsay together in the summer. It is comforting to note that what happened next is typical of the way things are organised in Argyll, even today. Symington Grieve boarded the steamer *Dunara Castle* at Greenock, and met Mr Malcolm McNeill, who was the brother of the proprietor, Major-General Sir John Carstairs McNeill, VC. In his brother's absence, Malcolm McNeill was willing to give permission to open the mound. So, on 22 June 1881 the excavation of Castail nan Gillean commenced. Another member of the team was Alexander Galletly, curator of the 'Museum of Science and Art' in Edinburgh.

These early excavations were approached systematically, and after three days the expedition had collected a quantity of shells, some bones, and some stone tools. These were taken to the Edinburgh museum, where they were examined by Dr R. H. Traquair, curator of the Natural History Department, and his assistant Mr John Gibson. These gentlemen soon identified one of the bones as the humerus of a great auk.

Galloway and Grieve returned to Oronsay in September, and soon discovered more great auk bones – eight in all – along with a vast quantity of other bones and shells. As the great auk bones were intermixed in a kitchen-midden with all the other remains, it was concluded that the birds must have bred on the numerous skerries around Oronsay, and had been hunted for food.

Historical references to birds on Colonsay and Oronsay are sparse. A charter of 1343 from David II to John, first Lord of the Isles, mentions peregrine falcons on some of the Hebridean islands, including Colonsay. Dean Monro commented on the large number of eider duck there in the 1540s, and also remarked on the presence of peregrine falcons. Pennant, in the 1770s, mentioned the eider, shelduck, barnacle geese, and choughs.

In *My Happy Hunting Grounds* (1914), Alfred Erskine Gathorne-Hardy has left an account of the halcyon days before World War I. He described how he visited the Laird, Sir John McNeill 'at home in his apartments at St James' Palace', in London, and arranged to rent Kiloran. After a short visit to Colonsay in the company of the Laird, a deal was done, and he returned in 1898 and 1899, spending August and September at Colonsay House – 'an ideal residence for a naturalist and sportsman'. At that time the old road from Scalasaig to Kiloran was still in use.

Quoting from his game book, Gathorne-Hardy offers us the result of his exertions:

	1898	*1899*
Partridges	50	105
Pheasants	10	2
Grouse	222	100
Hares	32	13
Rabbits	422	392
Woodcock	3	5
Black-game	64	68
Snipe	88	137

Wild duck	104	111
Various	55	112
	1,050	1,045

The 'wild duck' included eider, teal, widgeon, pochard and golden-eye.

FISH

All the species of sea fish common to the waters off the west of Scotland are found around Colonsay and Oronsay. Fishing off the rocks around the coast, or from the end of the pier at Scalasaig, lythe, mackerel, and saithe are commonly caught. Sea fishing and boat trips can be arranged locally. The only freshwater fish are eels and trout, which are found in the many small lochs and lochans. Loch Fada and Loch Sgoltaire give the best fishing. Boats are for hire on several of the larger lochs, but fishing from the bank is free to all visitors, who are asked to assist in conserving the natural stocks.

At the beginning of this century Gathorne-Hardy caught 1 to 1½lb trout in the lochs, and plaice, haddock, whiting, saithe and lythe in the sea.

Lobsters, prawns and crabs are caught locally by commercial fishermen. An oyster farm was established at Garvard around 1910, but according to Loder (1935) was 'defeated by the strength of the tide'. More recently, oyster beds have been established at the southern tip of Colonsay. The produce is marketed locally, as well as further afield – a big market has been developed for Colonsay oysters.

INSECTS

Very little work has been done on the hundreds of species of insects which live on Colonsay and Oronsay, though the Clarkes (1988) have identified some 300 beetles and more than 250 moths and butterflies. An unusual butterfly worthy of note is the Scots argus, which has been recorded on Colonsay. It is an Arctic butterfly which must have come to Scotland before the end of the Ice Age. It has not been seen recently, and its presence on Colonsay might be regarded as somewhat freakish.

Also rather unexpected is the presence of a native Australian landhopper, *Arcitalitrus dorrieni* (Crustacea: Amphipoda). The males range in size from 6 to 8mm (¼ to ⅓in); the females are from 10 to 12mm (⅖ to ½in). It lives in a damp habitat in leaf mould on the forest floor or in shaded ditches. It probably arrived accidentally about one hundred years ago among plants introduced into the gardens of Colonsay House. Recent research (Moore, P. G. and Spicer, J. I. : *Journal of Natural History*, 1986, **20**, 667–680) has shown it to be spreading at a minimum rate of 25m (82ft) year. It is also found in other parts of the British Isles: Cornwall, the Isles of Scilly, Dorset, and the Royal Botanic Gardens at Kew – more evidence of Colonsay's mild climate.

Regretfully, the species of *Insectivora* with which summer visitors will inevitably become most closely acquainted is a nasty, vicious little bug variously referred to as 'the scourge of the Highlands' or 'teeth with wings'. Their 'tackety boots' are a frequent topic of conversation. So tiny that it is impossible even to derive any satisfaction from despatching them, which is anyway an exercise in futility, the notorious and ubiquitous midge is one of the few unpleasant natural phenomena facing visitors to an otherwise idyllic natural environment.

As it is possible to take avoiding, if not remedial, action, it is better to face up to this threat to the tourist industry rather than gloss glibly over it. Midges (North Americans call them gnats) congregate in clouds, and swarm over anything edible, like a tourist, in large numbers. Reactions vary, but their bite can produce a weal like a wasp sting. They are inhaled, they crawl into your ears, eyes and nose, and generally make life totally unbearable. Open a car door and the car is instantly filled with midges. Midges thrive in damp, shady, calm conditions, and enjoy the line of decaying seaweed stranded by the high tides in March. They are so prevalent over such a large area of the Highlands and Islands that any thought of eradication is simply preposterous; the breeding grounds are too widespread and the ecological effects would be devastating. Various lotions and potions are marketed which claim to provide relief or to repel attacks, but it remains a strange fact that, whereas some individuals seem to be almost totally ignored, others are overwhelmed by clouds of midges apparently numbering in the millions. There are only two proven antidotes: wind and smoke. When having a picnic in a midgy area it is therefore best to reverse normal practice and choose somewhere breezy! Unfortunately lighting picnic fires to provide relieving smoke is not a practice to be encouraged on Colonsay, except perhaps on the beaches.

The hotel proprietor on Colonsay is of the opinion that the height above sea level at which midges operate is variable but predictable, depending on barometric pressure! It should thus be possible to follow a route which avoids them altogether. The flaw in this theory is that one may have to pass through the critical altitude at some point in the journey, whereupon clouds of midges will of course attach themselves to their victim and follow him.

Amongst the naturalists who have taken an interest in this species was Captain Peter Macfarlane, better known to posterity as 'Para Handy'. This master mariner, who successfully navigated his puffer the *Vital Spark* through the pages of the *Evening Times* of Glasgow seventy years ago, was the comic creation of the famous Scottish writer Neil Munro, whose capacity for serious writing should not be underestimated. But it is for Para Handy that he is most remembered.

In one of his most popular stories, 'Mudges', Para Handy's skill as a naturalist and ethnographer is evident, as he discusses different species of *Crustacea* and *Insectivora*. 'The best cockles in the country iss in Colonsay,' says Para Handy, 'but the people in Colonsay iss that slow they canna catch them. I was wance gatherin' cockles there, and the mudges were that large and bold, I had to throw stones at them.' It was also on Colonsay that a 'chenuine English towerist, wi' a capital red kilt', had a bad experience with midges: 'the first night on the island he went oot in his kilt, and came back in half an oor to the inns wi' his legs fair peetiful! There iss nothing that the mudges likes to see among them better than an English towerist with a kilt; the very tops wass eaten off his stockin's.' There seems to be little doubt that this anecdote was soundly based on the author's personal experience!

PLANTS

By 7500BC the post-glacial colonisation of the islands had produced a vegetational cover of birch-hazel scrub and woodland, with some elm and willow. By 4200BC there was also some oak, and stands of mixed alder and willow were widespread until 2000BC, at which time there is evidence from pollen analysis of scrub clearance and the development of grassland and pasture, with some arable activity. This all ties in well with what we know of the early human history of the islands, which will be discussed in chapter 4.

Today Colonsay and Oronsay are islands of great ecological and environmental contrasts. On the west side they are exposed to the full force of Atlantic gales, producing extensive areas of windswept, treeless moorland, heather moor, blanket bog, rough pasture and grassland, and coastal *machair*. By contrast, on the east side of Colonsay, there are small areas of dense mixed-deciduous woodland that support many warmth-demanding, frost-sensitive ferns, mosses, liverworts and lichens, suggesting conditions of high humidity and mild temperatures. Fraser Darling and Morton Boyd (1969) see Colonsay and Oronsay as 'an excellent example of islands which have the best of almost all worlds' and regard them as 'an epitome of the West Highland world in its full range of Atlantic exposure and sheltered mildness'.

There are two moderately large stands of semi-natural

woodland and scrub on the eastern coast of Colonsay, at Coille Mhor (NR410965) and Coille Bheag (NR417980). The Gaelic names mean 'the big wood' and 'the little wood'. These are scrubby woodlands of oak and hazel, with birch and willow in wet areas. Coille Bheag has been seriously damaged in recent years by burning and over-grazing, and Coille Mhor is botanically more interesting. It covers about 40 hectares (100 acres) and near the coast consists mainly of stunted, gnarled and twisted oak trees up to 8m (26ft) high with broad, spreading canopies. On higher ground a mixture of oak and birch grades into birch scrub. Aspen, rowan, holly and ash trees also occur. Grazing by sheep, cattle, goats and rabbits has produced rich grasslands, with many low-growing plants such as dog violet, yellow pimpernel, wood-sorrel, primrose, nightshade, and bugle, with the woodland itself carpeted with the bluebell or wild hyacinth. The woods have an extraordinarily rich flora of lichens, evidence that they are natural and ancient woodlands, occupying sites that have been continuously wooded for a very long time, probably from the postglacial colonisation of the islands. The fact that there is virtually no air pollution has protected these sensitive plants. The wood is now another SSSI, fenced under a management agreement to encourage regeneration. It should change rather dramatically in the next decade.

Several different species of ferns are found, of which a buckler fern with the smell of newly cut hay (*Dryopteris aemula*) is most notable. It is more usually associated with the Atlantic regions of southern Europe, like Madeira and the Azores, but it does well in Colonsay's mild, damp and almost frost-free climate.

On higher ground heather, blaeberry (blueberry) and bracken are widespread, with bog myrtle, pennywort, sphagnum mosses and water mint in boggy areas. In shaded, wet areas the golden saxifrage is common.

The most spectacular floral display on the islands is in May, when the *machair* which makes up most of Oronsay and the portions of Colonsay around Ardskenish, the Strand,

Kiloran and Balnahard burst into bloom. In *The Highlands and Islands* (1969) Fraser Darling and Morton Boyd give a list of sixty-six species of flowers and mosses commonly found in the *machair* – the natural coastal grassland on calcareous ground behind beaches – producing a green meadowland of sweet grass, giving excellent grazing for cattle. Moderate grazing adds organic fertiliser and keeps the sward clean; overgrazing and erosion caused by rabbits or by man can cause the catastrophic invasion of the *machair* by shifting sand dunes. The SSSI at Balnahard dunes will protect this dune system in the future.

The flowers of the *machair* blossom in order: white daisies, yellow buttercups, blue speedwell, purple clover, yellow birdsfoot trefoil, dandelions, silverweed, primrose, blue and yellow pansies, pink wild thyme, blue harebell, the tiny delicate white eyebright, and dozens more, drowning out the grass for a few weeks in an unforgettable blaze of colour. The sight and smell of the *machair* in full bloom is an unforgettable experience.

A slight mystery surrounds the question of whether the Scottish primrose (*Primula scotica*) is present on the islands. There is an unconfirmed report that it was spotted on the Ardskenish peninsula. It is not mentioned by Loder (1935), whose list of plant species collated all existing information and formed the basis for all future work. If it is present on Colonsay, it is well outside its normal range – the Northern Isles and the coast of the mainland as far south as Helmsdale, in Sutherland.

In former times, many plants were used for medicinal purposes, in cooking, or as dyes. For example, the lesser spearwort, abundant in marshy conditions, was used as a substitute for rennet in cheese-making, the roots of the white water lily produced a black dye, for wool and yarn, while the roots of tormentil were given to calves in milk as an astringent. The roots of silverweed, growing on the shoreline down to high water mark, were eaten raw or boiled like potatoes, as were also those of the heath vetch or heath pea (*Lathyrus montanus*). Stonecrop, pounded together with groundsel, was used to reduce swellings, especially on horses. The leaves of mugwort and coltsfoot were dried and used as a substitute for tobacco. Heather (*Calluna vulgaris*) was used extensively, for making doormats, brooms and ropes, or as a green dye, when mixed with alum. Loder (1935) says that heather ale was 'formerly made from the green tops' – interesting in view of the fact that traces of a heathery brew resembling whisky or mead have been found in pottery containers, dating to 2000BC, at an archaeological site on the Hebridean island of Rum.

In the last two chapters we have seen how the physical and natural environment of Colonsay and Oronsay developed. Into this environmental framework came the dominant Hebridean species, *Homo sapiens*. Over the last seven thousand years the inherited landscape has been altered by human interference. It is now time to look at the record of this process as it is preserved in the landscape, particularly in the stones and ruined walls so painfully and carefully erected in the ancient past. Our understanding of the changes in Colonsay and Oronsay over the millenia is closely linked to a study of the archaeology of the islands, with particular emphasis on their surviving monuments.

4 ARCHAEOLOGY AND EARLY HISTORY

For such a small island, Colonsay is particularly well-favoured with a good range of interesting prehistoric sites. Three cairns, eight standing stones, eight hut-circles, four ancient field systems, eight forts and thirteen duns, is indeed a formidable inventory for such a small place.

Oronsay, too, has good archaeology, with early shell mounds, a Bronze Age field system, an Iron Age hill-fort, and a magnificent medieval priory.

Although it is not strictly necessary in Scotland to ask for permission to visit archaeological sites or places of interest, whenever possible it is only common courtesy to inform farmers or property owners of your intentions. Particular care should be taken not to disturb stock, especially at lambing time, and of course fields under crops should be avoided. Gates should *always* be securely fastened, and care taken not to damage fencing. With a reasonable amount of common sense and courtesy, there should be no problem. But local folk do not appreciate visitors who behave badly, or arrogantly, and who fail to appreciate that making a living in these islands is a highly skilled and difficult undertaking.

It is illegal to undertake any form of excavation, including metal detecting, without a landowner's permission. In Scotland, *any* object recovered from the ground must be reported to the authorities and can be declared Treasure Trove by the Queen's and Lord Treasurer's Remembrancer, usually referred to in archaeological circles as the Q & LTR!

If this is done, financial compensation equal to the market value of the find will be paid to the finder. If not wanted for a national or local musuem, an object belongs to the *finder*. Failure to report objects found can result in prosecution. Anything found, including fragments of pottery, *should not be cleaned up*, but should be forwarded as soon as possible to the Royal Museum of Scotland, Queen Street, Edinburgh (tel 031 225 7534), formerly the National Museum of Antiquities of Scotland, for conservation and study. Amateur cleaning invariably detracts from the value of an object, as well as limiting research possibilities. Any human remains, of whatever age, *must* be reported to the police. These rules also apply to rivers and lochs, but objects found washed up on the shore or found underwater, for example on wrecks, should be reported to the Receiver of Wrecks.

Colonsay and Oronsay have been thoroughly investigated by the officers of the Royal Commission on the Ancient and Historical Monuments of Scotland, and their published *Inventory* gives a detailed catalogue of dozens of sites. Specialists are urged to consult a copy if possible – details will be found in the bibliography. Many of the archaeological sites are easy to visit, with a minimum of exertion. Some by their very nature are more difficult of access, but the dedicated enthusiast will have no trouble. In this book it is possible only to indicate the more important or spectacular sites; although many sites are described there are many others which, for reasons of poor preservation or inaccessibility, have had to be omitted.

MESOLITHIC HUNTERS: 7500–3500BC

Our knowledge of the earliest history of these islands, and indeed of the whole of the Hebrides, depends in large part on excavations conducted on Oronsay. In the last chapter we saw how Symington Grieve and William Galloway, starting in 1879, undertook excavations at Caisteal nan Gillean. Unfortunately Galloway's excavation notes have not survived, although it looks as though the undertaking was carried out in a careful and systematic way, given the constraints of the time. Grieve's interest was primarily in the natural history of the mound, and although he mentions some of the archaeological finds and illustrates some, their archaeological context is by no means clear. Barbed harpoon heads found in 1881–2 were exhibited at the International Fisheries Exhibition in 1883, but subsequently lost. However, sketches made at the time of the exhibition were published by Joseph Anderson in 1898 in the *Proceedings of the Society of Antiquaries of Scotland*. In this paper he also described excavations carried out by Galloway at two other shell mounds on Oronsay, but no other record of these excavations exists. Anderson must be given the credit for recognising the early date of these mounds.

For more than thirty years no further work appears to have been done, until the investigations of A. Henderson Bishop and Mungo Buchanan from 1910–13. This work is well documented; the finds, excavation papers and relevant correspondence are in the Hunterian Museum at the University of Glasgow. A hand-written report by Buchanan giving sixty pages of detailed notes on the 1911 excavations, with sketch plans, gives us much useful information. Even some photographs taken at the time have survived. The results of these excavations were published in *PSAS* in 1913–4. The main site dug was Cnoc Sligeach, which lies on the north-east corner of Oronsay.

The shell mounds then remained untouched until Dr Paul Mellars of the University of Cambridge carried out six seasons of investigations from 1970–79, using students from the universities of Cambridge and Sheffield. The data collected will form the basis of PhD dissertations for many years to come.

Although most of the evidence recovered by Mellars is environmental in nature, a great deal of more traditional archaeological material was recovered, even though most of the sites examined had been previously excavated. The main conclusion of the 1970's work is that the Oronsay sites were occupied, either continuously or intermittently, over a period of at least 600 to 700 years, from about 4100BC to 3400BC. The five different shell-midden sites investigated were spread around the coastline, and were shown to have been occupied at different seasons of the year. Analysis of the bone and shell remains provided a wealth of information about the habits and diet of the Mesolithic bands.

Much of the data collected by Mellars remains to be analysed, but already it is clear that in a European context Oronsay is one of the most important Mesolithic sites yet discovered. Amongst his more controversial hypotheses is the matter of whether Oronsay was more or less permanently inhabited by a small group of residents, or whether the island sites should rather be seen as what Mellars calls 'extraction camps' occupied 'by groups who returned – perhaps on a daily basis – to some residential base camp located either at a more central point in the interior of the island, or perhaps on one of the neighbouring islands such as Colonsay or Jura'.

Paul Mellars himself finds that the most intriguing question is this: why was a relatively small, isolated island like Oronsay colonised at all by Mesolithic groups, and why did an apparently intensive pattern of exploitation – after an interval of 600–700 years – come to such an abrupt end?

NEOLITHIC FARMERS: 3500–2000BC

Evidence for the presence of the first farmers on Colonsay and Oronsay is scanty, consisting only of leaf-shaped flint arrowheads from Druim Arstail, Oronsay. There are no examples on either island of the distinctive communal tombs known as chambered cairns, but the presence of six of these monuments on Islay and one on Jura does testify to the presence of Neolithic folk in the region. It may be that they visited Oronsay seasonally on hunting expeditions, like their Mesolithic predecessors, some of whom may still have been present in small numbers well into the third millennium BC.

BRONZE AGE SETTLERS: 2000–850BC

With the arrival of metal-working farmers and warriors soon after 2000BC, we are on safer ground, for they have left us a wide range of remains to study and to speculate about. Several Bronze Age cairns and cists have been uncovered in Colonsay and Oronsay, which have yielded human bones, cremations, pottery, flints, a bronze axe, and a bronze sword.

Unfortunately, no trace now remains of most of the stone-lined graves known in Scotland as 'cists' (pronounced 'kists'), found over the years at Colonsay House, Kiloran Bay, Lower Kilchattan, Machrins, Scalasaig and Uragaig. In 1846 'a stone coffin and human remains' were found while improvements were being made on the south-east side of Colonsay House. Martin Martin, writing at the end of the seventeenth century, records the discovery of 'two stone chests found lately in *Kil-ouran* Sands, which were composed of five stones each, and had human Bones in them'. Several cists have been uncovered at Lower Kilchattan, in 1856, 1870, 1881 and 1882, but any finds have not survived. However, a cast of a stone slab decorated with seven diamond or lozenge shapes is in the Royal Museum of Scotland in Edinburgh.

Similarly, the cists at Machrins noticed in 1920–1 were sketchily recorded, their precise location now unknown. A burial cist built of six slabs 60m (197ft) east of Colonsay Parish Church at Scalasaig was found in 1856, but a small urn found in it was left undisturbed and the site covered over.

Only at Uragaig can anything still be seen; the capstones of three cists discovered in 1882 about 120m (400ft) north of Creagan farmhouse are still visible (NR393981). The Early Bronze Age pottery type known as a food vessel was found in two cists, but a female skeleton, a flint knife, fragments of 'a very open textile fabric' and all the pottery are now lost.

However, a male skeleton laid out in a crouched position on the original floor-slab of one of the cists can be seen in the Museum of the Royal College of Surgeons in Edinburgh.

The remains of three cairns from this period can be seen in Colonsay. About 650m (2,135ft) east-south-east of Milbuie, on the northern end of a broad ridge (NR387929) are the remains of a large circular cairn, 16m (52½ft) in diameter, with a well-defined kerb of large boulders – a common Bronze Age type. Despite stone-robbing the cairn is still more than 1m (3ft) high; near its centre is a large stone slab which may be the capstone of a cist.

A smaller cairn is on the slopes of Càrnan Eòin (at NR407984). Several massive kerbstones are in place, and a large broken slab in the middle of the cairn may indicate a robbed cist.

A most unusual cairn can be found just outside Scalasaig, just to the east of the old road leading to Kiloran. Known as Buaile Riabhach, and marked on older maps as a stone circle, it is tiny, measuring 3.6m by 3m (12ft by 10ft) but is distinguished by the fact that two of the kerbstones are actually taller standing stones, their purpose clearly more than simply delineating the edge of the cairn. The larger stone is 2.3m (7½ft) in height – what James Wilson, on a tour of inspection for the Fishery Commissioners in 1841 called 'a Druidical pillar'. The other stone is leaning at an angle but would, if erect, be 1.5m (5ft) high. Excavated, or as modern archaeologists would say 'howked' in 1881, a dagger and sword were found. These were kept at Colonsay House, but are now lost.

This little cairn, easily visited, is located near the futuristic communications' dish operated by British Telecom. This juxtaposition, apparent to even the most casual observer, cannot help but remind us of some of the speculations and theories about standing stones and other antiquities. Is there any truth in the idea that standing stones were used to observe the movements of the sun, moon and stars? Did they function in some way as collectors of earth energy, or as communication devices of some kind? Is there any significance in their location – do ley lines exist? Although fringe archaeology can be great fun, it is probably a mistake to take it too seriously. But the Colonsay Hotel runs an annual 'ley line' competition, offering a prize for the most imaginative entry. Although this is organised in a light-hearted vein, every year entries are received from contenders who approach the subject enthusiastically, not to say obsessively. Needless to say, these make entertaining reading.

Not far from the little cairn at Buaile Riabhach is a more typical standing stone – a single, irregularly shaped stone pillar, 2m (6½ft) in height. It lies in a marshy hollow 60m (197ft) west of Scalasaig farmhouse. On the other side of the main road, 40m (130ft) west of the old track leading from Scalasaig to Milbuie, is another single stone only 1.1m (3½ft) high. Nearby is another stone which may be just a natural boulder. There are therefore three Bronze Age sites in a small area around Scalasaig.

Standing stones are found at several other locations on Colonsay. None survive on Oronsay, although as we shall see, it seems certain that Bronze Age folk settled and farmed there. The most spectacular stones are at Drumclach ('the ridge of the stones'), 70m (230ft) north-east of Lower Kilchattan farmhouse. Here are 'two great erect stones monumental', visited by Thomas Pennant in 1772, known locally as 'Fingal's Limpet Hammers'. Fingal is the great hero of Irish epic literature, immortalised in the English-speaking world by Mendelssohn. As befitting his larger-than-life status the stones are perceived as having been used by him to knock limpets off rocks. The shape of the stones is, of course, very like that of the small stone tools found in the Oronsay middens, and still used locally to dislodge shellfish. The standing stones, aligned NNW-SSE, are near the site of the cists uncovered last century. Clearly this area was of considerable ritual and ceremonial importance in the Bronze Age. There is, however, no evidence that the Drumclach stones are the remnants of a stone circle. Although single stones are more common, it is not at all unusual for two or three stones to occur in a line – many examples could be cited.

Two single stones can be visited near Balnahard, at the north end of Colonsay. One is known as Clach a'Pheanais, and lies 50m (164ft) north-east of a ruined chapel and burial ground. It stands 1.25m (4ft) high, aligned east to west, with a straight edge to the west and its east side curving up to a flat top. Its name means 'the stone of penance', and there is a tradition that it was used for flagellation by a community of nuns. About 1.1km (⅔ mile) east of Balnahard farmhouse, on the south-west slopes of Cnoc a'Charraigh ('the hill of the standing stone'), there is a stone 1.4m (4½ft) high, aligned east to west, rising with straight sides to a pointed top. Beside it is a 2m (6½ft)-long stone slab, probably a fallen standing stone.

At the opposite end of the island, near Garvard, is a stone pillar on the rocky knoll called Cnoc Eibriginn. It may not be prehistoric, as this site is associated with the administration of local justice in medieval times, and the stone may not be quite in its original position, having fallen by 1944 and been re-erected in about 1960.

A standing stone appearing on a 1900 Ordnance Survey map was once located 450m (1,480ft) east of Machrins, but it has now disappeared. It is not clear whether it was a pre-historic stone, or perhaps associated with the nearby chapel of Kilbride, of which there is also now no trace. Similar ambiguity surrounds 'MacFie's Stone', Carraig Mhic a'Phi, at Baleruminmore (NR384914), which may be a prehistoric standing stone that has been 'Christianised'. This monument will be discussed in chapter 5.

Cup-and-ring markings are one category of Bronze Age monument common on the adjacent mainland of Argyll but for some reason much rarer on the islands and represented on Colonsay by a single example. On a boulder at the mouth of the cave of Uamh na Mine (NR404985), at the northern end of Kiloran Bay, are two cup marks, 60mm (2⅓in) in diameter by 40mm (1½in) in depth. We do not know the meaning of these symbols, nor how they were used.

There are no prehistoric stone circles, in the archaeological sense, on Colonsay and Oronsay, despite misleading statements in some older books. There are, however, several circular stone structures, dating probably from the Bronze Age. As their date and function has only recently been recognised by the authoritative Royal Commission on the Ancient and Historical Monuments of Scotland (RCAHMS), past writers can perhaps be forgiven for describing them wrongly.

An extensive Bronze Age field-system, with hut-circles, stone walls and stock enclosures lies on Beinn Arnicil (NR373918), to the west of the road from Scalasaig to the Strand, and north of the medieval chapel called Teampull a'Ghlinne. Here we are closer to the everyday life of Bronze Age farmers than at the burial cairns, cists and standing stones, which though obviously important in their social system, must have been used or visited only occasionally.

We know that this field-system must date from the Bronze Age (or before) because of the peat which now covers the hill, almost submerging the field-boundaries and enclosures. As we saw in chapter 2, this peat started to accumulate *after* the climatic deterioration which took place at the end of the Bronze Age, from about 1200BC onwards. Recent excavations on Islay and Jura at similar sites have yielded radiocarbon dates of 1800–1200BC, while pollen analysis on Islay has provided evidence of cereal cultivation.

The field boundaries on Beinn Arnicil are made of stony heaps incorporating closely spaced upright slabs. Just below the summit cairn of the hill is a large pear-shaped enclosure built in the same way, using particularly large stones. For this reason it has been interpreted as a ceremonial stone circle, but the RCAHMS insist that 'there is no reason to believe that it does not form part of the field system', and so it is now understood to be a stock enclosure, presumably for cattle. Other, smaller enclosures are scattered over the hill.

To the south of the large pear-shaped enclosure is a

complex of stony ruins that is the remains of a Bronze Age farmstead. Although unexcavated, it is very similar to hut-circles explored by the RCAHMS in other parts of Argyll.

On the eastern edge of the Beinn Arnicil field system, near the road, is an Iron Age dun, Dùnan nan Con, which will be described below. Just to its west is a long, rectangular building, presumably the ruins of a nineteenth century farmstead. There is therefore evidence for more or less continuous settlement and farming in this area for 3,500 years.

Other single hut-circles have been noted at Balnahard (NR413998), Beinn Bheag (NR405986), Corr Dhùnan (NR384951), Druim nam Faoileann (NR359960), Gleann Raonabuilg (NR372939), Kiloran (NR399962) and Tòrr an Tuirc (NR381960). Another extensive field-system, with

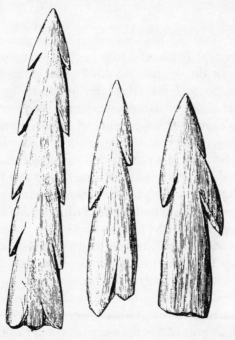

Three harpoon heads of bone from Caisteal-nan-Gillean, Oronsay

banks and clearance cairns, lies south-west of Garvard farm-house, while fragmentary remains of ten others have been noted around the island.

Oronsay, too, was farmed in the Bronze Age. An extensive prehistoric field-system has been recognised on Druim Mór, the broad peninsula that forms the south-west limb of the island. Here, there is a well-preserved hut-circle, and all around it are field clearance cairns, stony banks, and larger cairns, some possibly for burials, with the ridge-and-furrow signs of cultivation everywhere – some of it possibly comparatively recent.

Stray finds of pottery and metalwork from Colonsay and Oronsay confirm that the islands were settled throughout the Bronze Age. The Early Bronze Age flat-axe from Loch Fada and the Late Bronze Age sword from Beinn nan Guidairean illustrate this point.

THE IRON AGE: 600BC–400AD

Without necessarily assuming a wholesale population change, it is clear that the prehistoric way of life in the islands had changed by about 600BC. For the first time we have folk who used iron for tools and weapons. We now find large stone-walled forts serving as the nucleus of settlements, as compared with the very 'open' character of Bronze Age settlements. It is wrong to imagine that the entire population lived on fortified hilltops all the time, but their leaders and their families and retinues probably did, and in times of danger the forts would have been used to shelter and protect the local population.

Archaeological research into the problem of different types of Iron Age fortifications in Argyll is in its infancy, due mainly to lack of excavation. Archaeological excavation is an expensive and painstakingly slow business. Only one single Iron Age hill-fort in Argyll has been explored in modern times, from dozens of known examples, and this excavation, at Bealloch Hill, near Campbeltown on the Kintyre peninsula, raised more questions than it answered! There, evidence for Neolithic hilltop occupation was found, and two Bronze Age cremation burials were found sealed underneath the inner rampart of the hill-fort, of which only about 25% was excavated after three seasons of digging. The logistical problems involved in excavating on a Hebridean island are obvious. To make matters worse, probably at least 1m (more than 3ft) of rubble would have to be cleared from the interior of any Iron Age site on Colonsay before occupation levels would be reached.

It is therefore exceedingly foolhardy to approach the subject too dogmatically, or with any expectation other than a few cautious generalities. Following traditional terminology, the RCAHMS recognise two main classes of Iron Age fortifications, which they call 'forts' and 'duns'. Generally speaking, 'forts' are large enough to accommodate an entire local population, are built of one or more drystone walls encircling a hilltop, and are thought to date from about 850BC (on the mainland) to about 100BC. By contrast, a 'dun' (pronounced 'doon', from the Gaelic word meaning 'fort'!) is typically a small circular stone-walled structure built on a rocky knoll, large enough to accommodate only a single extended family, and dating usually from 100BC to AD200.

Using this classification, there are eight forts and thirteen duns on Colonsay, and a single fort on Oronsay. Some of these sites were re-occupied in the Middle Ages, long after their abandonment at the end of the Iron Age, and feature in the history of the islands at that time. Their Gaelic names derive from later times, and not too much should be read into the meaning of these names when dealing with these sites in a prehistoric context.

FORTS

Just to the west of Scalasaig, the fort of Dùn Éibhinn (Dunevin) is the most accessible, most interesting, and best preserved prehistoric site on the islands (NR382943). Access is gained to the hill at the back of Scalasaig farmhouse, from where it is an easy walk across to the site, which is, however, very steep-sided.

There are two defensive walls around the site. One follows the edge of the summit plateau, enclosing an area 20m by 18m (65 by 59ft). Some 6.5m (21ft) below, along the edge of a natural terrace, a second wall encloses the site, except on the north-west, where the steepness of the rock is defence enough. Entrances through both walls are visible at the north-eastern corner.

Traces of oblong and rectangular buildings on the summit are likely to be vestiges of medieval occupation, and the remains of buildings round the base of the knoll are also likely to be medieval or later. From a sixteenth-century grave slab at Iona we know that Malcolm MacDuffie, 'Lord of Dunevin in Colonsay', lived here, but of the Iron Age inhabitants we know nothing.

Martin Martin records that 'the Natives have a Tradition among them, of a very little Generation of People, that lived once here, call'd *Lusbirdan*, the same with *Pigmies*.' It is possible that this tradition preserves a folk-memory of the Bronze Age population, or even of the Mesolithic hunter/gatherers who may have lived on in the islands long after the arrival of incomers bringing their new technology and their new culture.

The site commands extensive views over the southern half of Colonsay, and is well worth a visit. Suggestions that there may have been a moat or wet ditch around Dùn Éibhinn are now regarded as fanciful.

At the south end of Colonsay is Dùn Cholla (NR377915), easily reached from the track leading to Baleruminmore. A single stone wall encloses an area 54m by 25m (177ft by 82ft). The southern and western sides are protected by sheer cliffs; on the north-east, where the approach is over a gentle grassy slope, the wall is particularly strong – up to 6m (20ft) thick. The entrance, on the north-east, is quite well preserved and it can be seen that it has been modified by the addition of

stones to make it narrower. Traces of enclosures of comparatively recent date can be seen inside. There is a fine view over
the Strand.

The name means 'the fort of Coll', and it has often
been put forward as the residence of the possibly apocryphal
Kolbein after whom some authorities argue that the island of
Colonsay gets its name. But in any case, Dùn Cholla is clearly
an Iron Age fort, which must predate the arrival of Kolbein
by several centuries.

Martin Martin mentions that 'there are several forts here,
one of which is call'd *Duncoll*; it is near the middle of the Isle,
it hath large Stones in it, and the Wall is seven Foot broad'. It
is therefore likely that this name, and 'Dun-Evan', date from
at least the twelfth century, if not before. It is difficult to
estimate the disruption to place-names caused by the Viking
occupation.

At Dùn Gallain (NR348931), on the rocky promontory west
of the golf course at Machrins, traces of two stone walls can
be seen. As at Dùn Éibhinn, one encloses the summit area,
30m by 20m (98ft by 65ft) while an outer wall lower down
surrounds the rocky summit knoll on three sides; on the north
side sheer cliffs make any secondary defence unnecessary. The
entrance, poorly preserved, is to the north-east. There are no
traces in the interior of any prehistoric buildings. The name
means 'the fort of the strangers' and is quite a common name
for this kind of site. It is often taken as referring to the Vikings,
and is in exactly the kind of place where Norse raiders might
have set up a base when visiting the island.

Dùn Meadhonach (NR414999), the 'middle fort', is 530m
(1,740ft) north of Balnahard farmhouse, on the summit of
a rocky ridge. It is in a very ruinous state; its interior is
featureless, apart from the foundations of three secondary
circular structures on the north-western side, overlying the
fort wall. The summit area, 55m by 24m (180ft by 78ft), is
enclosed by a single stone wall, but a terrace to the north-east
is also enclosed.

These four forts are all on the summit of a rocky knoll or

ridge, with a reasonably flat area enclosed by a stone wall. Oronsay's one Iron Age site, the fort of Dùn Dòmhnuill (NR354890), is also of this type. This fort, the name of which suggests some association with Donald, grandson of Somerled (see chapter 5), lies 450m (1,495ft) east of Oronsay Priory, and 150m (490ft) north of the farm track leading from the Strand to Oronsay House. The site is a classic *roche moutonnée*, sculptured by ice. A single stone wall encloses an area 69m by 24m (225ft by 78ft) with precipitous drops on three sides. At the east side, where the entrance must have been, the defences are strengthened by an outwork enclosing a terrace 3.5m (11½ft) below the fort wall. Pottery sherds in the Hunterian Museum at the University of Glasgow make it clear that this was originally an Iron Age site, whatever its later associations, real or imaginary. The name, and the presence of a stone basin carved into a rocky outcrop in the interior, often associated with inauguration ceremonies in the Dark Ages (Early Historic Period) testify to a possible secondary period of occupation. The foundations of two oval huts overlying the collapsed fort wall may also date from this period, or later.

Quite a different type of Iron Age defensive structure, the promontory fort, is represented by three examples on Colonsay. In these cases the concept is to build one or more stone walls across the neck of a coastal promontory, further defence being provided by precipitous cliffs. These sites are all very ruinous, and downright dangerous to visit, especially in wet or windy conditions. Needless to say, children should be closely supervised.

The best is Dùn Uragaig (NR381982), on the coast south-west of Kiloran Bay, where a narrow neck of land is defended by a stone wall 2m (6½ft) thick. The entrance is centrally located, and on either side of it, built against the wall, are the remains of circular huts. Traces of seven structures can be made out, including a small platform 4m (13ft) in diameter. The cliffs, which provide a habitat for nesting sea birds, fall 30m (98ft) to the sea on all sides.

A little to the north of Dùn Uragaig is Dùn Tealtaig (NR389983), overlooking the western end of Kiloran Bay. The site is surrounded by sheer cliffs, except on the south-west, where access is easy. Various features in the interior include small enclosures, scooped platforms and terraces.

On the rugged north-west coast of Colonsay, 1.5km (almost a mile) north-west of Colonsay School, is another promontory fort, Meall Lamalum (NR368969). Here two ruinous stone walls defend a neck of land. Just inside the entrance, at the north end of the inner wall, is a hut site, with the remains of three other circular huts in the interior of the site.

No trace now remains of a fort supposedly located on Beinn Eibhne, known as Dùn Mara. Recorded in 1881 as an arc of wall about .6m (2ft) thick, erosion has obliterated it completely. At least, the RCAHMS field-workers could not find it.

DUNS

Only a few of Colonsay's thirteen duns are worth a visit, except for the archaeological specialist. Some are so ruinous that even an expert could be excused for not being able to locate them without the kind of detailed instructions provided by the RCAHMS in their published inventory of ancient monuments on the islands.

Dùnan nan Con (NR377920), although ruinous, has already been mentioned as lying on the very edge of the Beinn Arnicil Bronze Age field-system, and as it lies only a few yards west of the main road, it should be visited. A low band of stony rubble encloses an area 16m by 11m (52ft by 36ft), the entrance indicated only by a gap in the rubble. The fine facing stones which would once have made up the wall, which would probably have been 4 to 5m (13 to 16ft) in height, have all been plundered, leaving only the vestiges of a site, exceedingly unspectacular even to the untrained eye. This is, alas, all too typical of the state of preservation of Iron Age sites. Internal structures would have been built of wood, thatch, wattle and daub, all long decayed, and now recoverable only by excavation.

Slightly better preserved is Dùnan nan Nighean (NR415976), a D-shaped structure situated in an area of rough moorland 2.2km (1⅓ miles) north-east of Colonsay House and 250m (820ft) west of Port a'Bhuailtein. It lies on the southern edge of the woodland of Coille Bige described in chapter 3. Even in the Iron Age, it must have seemed remote and isolated. The name means 'the fort of the maidens' (young girls), suggesting female isolation for safety, childbearing, or for some puberty ritual – all ideas found in societies in different parts of the world today. But it is very dangerous to attribute Celtic ideas about how these sites were used to their Iron Age inhabitants, about whom the Gaelic-speaking immigrants of the fifth century AD and later knew nothing.

At Dùnan nan Nighean, some of the lintels over the entrance passage are still in place. Iron Age pottery found in a 1949 excavation is in the Royal Museum of Scotland.

Near Ardskenish (NR347911), 320m (1,050ft) south-east of the farmhouse, are the remains of a roughly rectangular dun, 15m by 5m (50ft by 10ft), overlooking the shore. This is a beautiful part of the island, with interesting geology, and the dun, although ruinous, is well worth a visit.

For the enthusiast, Dùnan Leathan (NR381934), 280m (920ft) NNW of Milbuie, and the dun at Tobar Fuar (NR357938), overlooking the shore at the north-east end of Machrins Bay, are worth a look. The dun at Queen's Bay (NR389933) is notable for its size – it is one of the smallest recorded, measuring only 5.5m by 4m (18ft by 13ft).

This necessarily brief survey of archaeological sites on Colonsay and Oronsay will, I hope, whet the appetite of the visitor or armchair traveller. Further information on Scottish archaeology in general and island sites in particular can be found in the bibliography at the end of this book.

5   MONKS AND VIKINGS

We know very little about the situation in the Hebrides at the end of the Iron Age. As we enter what used to be called the 'Dark Ages', now more optimistically called the 'Early Historic Period', we are at the dawn of history in Colonsay and Oronsay. That is to say, we have reached a time when *written* records, though scanty, are finally available.

Perhaps as early as the third century AD, people from the northern coast of Ireland, called 'Scotti' by the Romans, started to make their way across the short stretches of water separating them from the coastline of a country that would later bear their name – Scotland. Exactly how this movement of people took place is not known, though scholars now dismiss the idea of a mass invasion and talk instead of cultural diffusion, shared lineage, and élite dominance.

COLUMBA

In AD563 the Irish cleric known in his own land as Calum Cille and in Scotland today as Columba, sailed into exile with twelve followers. Exactly where he went, and when, is the subject of jealous disputation in different parts of Argyll. We do know he ended up on the island of Iona, where he established a community.

Recent research has tended to emphasise the political aspects of his enterprise, as a corrective to the missionary image familiar to all Scottish schoolchildren. For Columba's reason for converting the Picts to Christianity had as much to do with safeguarding the new kingdom of Dalriada as it did with concern for the mortal souls of the heathen Picts.

We know that by AD560 something approaching a separate political framework had been established in Argyll – the very name means 'the extent or boundary of the Gael'. This society was controlled by people related to the ruling families of Ireland. Columba, himself of royal blood, was a useful agent in Dalriada's need to consolidate their position in Argyll.

It is felt that he must have gone to Iona with the agreement of the ruler of Dalriada, and that it is inconceivable that he went there directly without clearing it first with the political authorities, as it were. Thus it appears, as always seemed likely, that the tales about Columba making his way north from Ireland, stopping off at various islands until he could no longer see the coastline of his native land, are spurious history. It is far more likely that he was granted Iona and told that he could establish his community there, thus reinforcing Dalriada's claim to the islands off the west coast.

There is a story that Columba landed on Oronsay but, since he could still see the coastline of Ireland from the summit of Beinn Oronsay, re-embarked and sailed further north, to Iona. In support of this story, it is pointed out that there is a well dedicated to Columba on Colonsay. Tobar Chaluim Chille ('Columba's well') lies beyond the north-east end of Kiloran Bay (at NR404986), and is quite an impressive little structure. Its slab lintels and rough corbelling enclose a chamber roughly 30cm (1ft) deep. The water, which is crystal clear, is reputed to have healing properties. It is certainly deliciously refreshing to drink. There are many coins in the well, thrown into it for good luck. It is not easy to find, but is best approached by following the Balnahard track up the hill from the end of Kiloran Bay. From the top of the hill, where the track levels out, it is about 200m (655ft) to the site of the well, which lies in a narrow gulley some 30m (100ft) down the slope to the west of the track. A bronze chalice is provided for the benefit of thirsty visitors, installed by the hotel proprietor and inscribed with a Gaelic proverb: TU GLUAIS FAICILLEACH LE CUPAN LAN, meaning 'Go warily

Kiloran beach at low tide

Conservation area, Balnahard

(*Above*) Mesolithic shell
mound, Oronsay (before
excavation)

(*Left, top*) Mesolithic shell
mound, Oronsay, looking
towards Islay and Jura

(*Left, middle*) Cnoc an
eadraiginn, Garvard

(*Left, bottom*) Dun
Domhnuill, Oronsay

(*Right*) Standing stone,
Scalasaig, with Dun
Eibhinn in the background

Oronsay Priory

Medieval chapel, Cill Chaitriona, Balnahard

Church of Scotland, Scalasaig

Baptist Church, Kilchattan

View of Scalasaig from above Dun Eibhinn

Isle of Colonsay Hotel

Blackface sheep, Garvard

(*Overleaf*) Cliff scenery near Dun Uragaig, Colonsay.
(*Royal Commission on Ancient Monuments, Scotland*)

Farmyard scene, Scalasaig

(Left) Medieval grave-slab of Bricius MacMhuirich, Oronsay Priory.
(Royal Commission on Ancient Monuments, Scotland)

(Right) Effigy of Prior Donaldus MacDuffie, Oronsay.
(Royal Commission on Ancient Monuments, Scotland)

(*Above, left*) Ruined cottage, Drumclach

(*Above, right*) Memorial to Donald MacKinnon, Kilchattan

'Fingal's Limpet Hammers', Kilchattan, Colonsay

The Standing Stone at
Garvard, Colonsay.
*(Royal Commission on
Ancient Monuments,
Scotland)*

The MacDuffie strong-
hold of Dun Eibhinn,
near Scalasaig.
*(Royal Commission on
Ancient Monuments,
Scotland)*

Dunan nan Nighean fort,
Colonsay, from the
south west.
(*Royal Commission on
Ancient Monuments,
Scotland*)

Oronsay Cross from the
west. (*Royal Commission
on Ancient Monuments,
Scotland*)

Oronsay Priory as seen by Pennant, late 18th century.
(Royal Commission on Ancient Monuments, Scotland)

Jura at Scalasaig Harbour, 1870.
(Royal Commission on Ancient Monuments, Scotland)

Post Office Landrover crossing the Strand to Oronsay

Crossing the Strand, 1937. *(Courtesy of Miss E. B. Rennie)*

Kiloran Mill, interior

Portable scales from a Viking burial at Kiloran Bay, Colonsay.
(Royal Commission on Ancient Monuments, Scotland)

with a full cup'. He acquired this vessel in a metal market in Bhaktapur, in Nepal, in the hills beyond Kathmandu!

Of course, wells dedicated to Columba are common throughout the West Highlands and Islands, and the existence of this well on Colonsay is certainly no proof that Columba ever set foot there. However, the very presence of the well, and its dedication to the most powerful saint of the Celtic church, suggests the possibility that it may date from pre-Christian times. Wells were significant in prehistoric times, and we have already seen that Colonsay and Oronsay were well populated in the Iron Age. It is certainly an intriguing idea, but as is often the case, we can never be sure. The well in the grounds of Colonsay House, Tobar Odhrain ('the well of Oran'), is another candidate for this line of thinking. The little stone beside this well, which has a cruciform carving surmounted by a carved head, is Irish in design and dates from the seventh or eighth century. It was brought to the grounds of Colonsay House in 1870 from the burial ground at Riasg Buidhe.

ORAN

There is a persistent local tradition that the islands were visited by Oran, another saint of the early Celtic church. Some support is lent to this idea by the place-name Kiloran, suggesting an Early Christian complex in the area, and by the presence of an Early Christian chapel on the island of Oronsay.

Having dismissed the idea in chapter 1 that Oronsay is named after St Oran, but derives instead from 'Orfiris-ey', the Norse for 'a tidal island', it is nevertheless necessary to record that there is strong local feeling to the contrary. The fact that there are many other 'Oronsays' in the Hebrides, all tidal islands, cuts no ice with the local population, who strongly believe in the Oran connection and have taken to spelling the name 'Oransay'.

They may well be right. But this rather aggressive

orthographic attitude cannot really be justified. Spelling is notoriously variable in old documents, and usually amounts only to phonetic rendering of a name, often with laughable results. Oronsay itself ('or Oransay', if you prefer) is rendered variously as Oruansei (1203), Orwansay (1353), Orwnsay (1382), Orbkansa (1426), Orwinsai (1492), Oruansay (1549), Orransay (1554), Orasai (1555), Oronsey (1558), Orvinsay (1592), Orsay (c1600), Oronsay (1616), Orvonsa (1654), Oransay (1687). This list is by no means exhaustive.

In a charter given by John, Lord of the Isles in 1469, the lands of Oronsay, North Uist are granted, amongst others, to his brother Hugh. The spelling of the name in this document as 'Orvinsaig' lends credence to the Norse derivation of the word. At the risk of causing offence, I prefer the 'official' Ordnance Survey spelling in this book. It is possible that Oran *did* visit the islands, giving his name to Kiloran, and that in the later Middle Ages, after the Vikings had come and gone, local memory of his visit caused the alteration of the Norse name. Equally, it is possible that the name 'Kiloran' was 'invented' in the late Middle Ages and applied to Colonsay in the belief that the church of Oronsay was founded by Oran, who travelled extensively in the Western Isles and is commemorated in many dedications and place-names.

EARLY CHURCHES

There is, moreover, the Early Christian chapel on Oronsay, dedicated to St Mary. Cill Mhoire (Kilmory) is a tiny, turf-covered, round-angled structure, aligned east-west, lying 80m (263ft) south of the track to Oronsay Priory, near where it turns due west after crossing the Strand (NR360888).

Another Cill Mhoire, also evidently Early Christian in date (that is, between AD563 and c850), can be found in Colonsay, at Upper Kilchattan, 90m (295ft) east-north-east of the Baptist Chapel. Similar in appearance to the Oronsay chapel, the drystone walls are slightly better preserved. It is surrounded by a D-shaped enclosure (NR377957).

Another enclosure, but not the chapel, survives at Bale-ruminmore, Colonsay (NR384914). There is a small oblong building on the site, but the RCAHMS view it as 'probably associated with the later agricultural use of the site', based partly on its appearance and on the position of the entrance, which is in the centre of the south wall.

An Early Christian date for the enclosure is indicated by two cross-decorated stones found at the site. One of the stones, known as Carraig Mhic a' Phi ('MacFie's stone'), stands within a small railed enclosure. There are plaques commemorating its re-erection by the Clan MacPhee Society in 1977. Apart from the fact that Malcolm MacDuffie, the last chief of the clan, was put against the stone and shot in 1623, it really has nothing to do with MacPhees, being a typical cross-decorated stone of Early Christian date. Indeed, the possibility of it being a prehistoric standing stone, its magic destroyed by the addition of a carved cross, as happened elsewhere, has already been mentioned.

In recent times this stone has had an eventful history. It was damaged by cattle in 1918, re-erected in 1934, and knocked down again by 1960. The broken pieces were re-assembled, and in 1977 it was placed in its present position, with its protective enclosure. Unfortunately, despite consultation with the correct government department, it was put up literally upside down and back to front, so that the decorative cross carving is now mostly embedded in concrete. As a photograph taken about 1870 and published by Loder (1935) was easily available, this mistake was avoidable. The whole episode, regrettable to say the least, illustrates the dangers of ill-informed amateur enthusiasm. Unhappily the archaeological authorities in Edinburgh do not always provide enthusiastic locals with the encouragement and support they deserve, and when faced with interminable procrastination and red tape it is easy to succumb to the temptation to get on with the job without bureaucratic interference. The story surrounding Malcolm MacFie's demise, and the later medieval history of the islands, will be described in chapter 6.

At the north end of Colonsay, half a mile north-east of Balnahard farm, is the chapel and enclosed burial ground of Cill Chaitriona (NR421998), dedicated to St Catherine of Alexandria – Caitriona in Gaelic. At the north-west corner of the enclosure stands a crude stone slab 0.88m (nearly 3ft) in height, carved into the shape of a cross. It is badly worn through cattle using it as a rubbing post, and conceivably

Rough sketch of the MacFie's stone, Pairc na h'eaglais, Baleruminmore, Colonsay. Taken in 1880

may have had more decorative carving originally. In the Royal Museum of Scotland, Edinburgh, another carved stone from this site can be seen, with unusual decoration – four holes pierce the slab to enhance the carving of the cross.

Loder (1935) mentions the tradition that this site was a nunnery. A broad, sloping stone to the north of the enclosure is known as Clach a'Pheanais, 'the stone of penance', and was supposedly used for flagellation. It is described in chapter 4 as a possible Bronze Age standing stone.

No trace now remains of a chapel, possibly Early Christian, near Ardskenish, dedicated to St Coinnech (Kenneth). Two human burials were found near Cill Choinnich (NR355916) in about 1880. Also now disappeared completely is the chapel and burial ground of Cill Bhride (Kilbride), located somewhere to the east of Machrins farmhouse. According to Loder (1935) it was dismantled by a farmer in 1881. A cross-marked stone from this site now stands in a field 100m (325ft) south of Machrins farm. The dedication is to the Irish saint Bridget or Bride (Gaelic Brighid). Martin Martin, writing in about 1700, gives an account of how St Bridget's Eve (February 2nd) was celebrated:

The mistress and servants of each family take a sheaf of oats and dress it up in woman's apparel, put it in a large basket and lay a wooden club by it, and this they call Briid's bed; and then the mistress and servants cry three times, 'Briid is come! Briid is welcome!' This they do just before going to bed, and when they rise in the morning they look among the ashes, expecting to see the impression of Briid's club there. Which, if they do, they reckon is a true presage of a good crop and prosperous year and the contrary they take as an ill-omen.

This extract speaks volumes about the superstitions of

Viking brooch from Carn-nan-Bharraich, Oronsay

the inhabitants and the survivability of ancient, even pre-Christian customs.

VIKINGS

After having been established in the area for 250 years, the Christian church faced its most serious challenge – Viking raiders. On Iona, monks were slaughtered and the monastery pillaged. Columba's relics and the illuminated book thought to be in his own hand were taken to Kells in Ireland for safe keeping.

By AD850 to 900, the raiding parties were being replaced by Norse settlers who came to the islands with their wives, families, stock and seed corn, and took over the better farmland. For the next 300 years Colonsay and Oronsay were ruled by the Norse, until the great guerrilla leader Somerled liberated them in the 1150s.

The Norsemen have left a permanent mark on the landscape in two ways. Firstly, Viking burials have turned up in sand-dune sites – six in Colonsay and five in Oronsay. Secondly, many Norse place-names survive, still in daily use more than eight hundred years after Norse rule was overthrown. Names such as Ardskenish, Loch Staosnaig, Oronsay, Scalasaig, Sgreadan, Turnigil, and others, are a daily reminder of Norse influence.

Sadly, there is nothing to be seen at any of the Viking burial sites, but material from them can be seen in museums in Glasgow and Edinburgh, amounting to over fifty objects in all. The finest came from burials in the sand dunes at Kiloran Bay, explored in 1882–3. A rectangular enclosure built of stone slabs and measuring 4.6m by 3.1m (15ft by 10ft) contained the crouched burial of a man. Finds included an iron sword, a spearhead, an axehead, a silver pin, bits of an elaborate horse harness, and a portable balance with scales and seven decorated weights. Probably it is the grave of an itinerant merchant and metalworker. Similar scales have been found on the island of Gigha, and at many other sites throughout Europe visited by Scandinavian adventurers. Boat rivets at the Kiloran burial were thought to suggest not a boat-burial, but possibly the use of an upturned hull as a roof for the enclosure, which would have been covered over with earth and sand. The skeleton of a horse lay outside the enclosure.

In the sand dunes west of Machrins, a Viking burial was discovered in 1891, producing a sword, shield fragments, a spearhead, an amber bead, a bronze pin, a

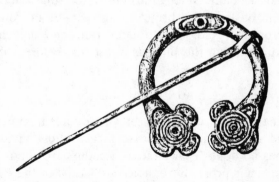

Penannular brooch found at Machrins, Colonsay, in 1891

(*Above*) Bronze pin with moveable ring-head and
(*below*) bronze belt-mounting, both found at Ardskenish, Colonsay,
in 1891

penannular (almost ringlike) brooch and fragments of horse
harness.

Traces of a small Viking-age settlement were exposed
by erosion of the *machair* 1km (⅔ mile) west of Machrins
in 1977, and excavated. Finds included iron knives, bone
pins and needles, a saddle quern (for grinding grain), stone
pounders, and animal bones: cattle, sheep, pig and roe deer.
An adjoining burial produced human bones and the skeleton
of a small dog, laid in the grave with its head on the knees of
the human skeleton. Among the finds were a ring-headed pin,
a fragment of decorated bronze, fragments of an iron knife
and an iron nail. Radiocarbon dates from the Machrins material indicated that the site was in use just before AD800.

MAGNUS BARELEGS

Something of the ambience of those violent times can
be found in the pages of Norse sagas, whose vivid (and
sometimes no doubt exaggerated) accounts are almost journalistic in their prose. Several accounts exist of the exploits
of Magnus Barelegs in the Hebrides in the 1090s, and it can be

assumed there were many other raiders, now forgotten, who engaged in similar activities. The account in the *Heimskringla* is typical:

And when Magnus came to the Hebrides he began at once to plunder and burn the inhabited lands, and he slew the menfolk. And they robbed everything wherever they went. But the people of the land fled far and wide; some to Scotland's firths, some south to Kintyre, or over to Ireland. Some received quarter and did homage.

Using the typically flowery style of the sagas, redolent with vivid figures of speech, the storyteller, in this case Bjorn Cripplehand, summarises Magnus's campaign in language to-day reserved for the sporting pages of tabloid newspapers:

The branch-scorcher played greedily up into the sky in Lewis; there was far and wide an eager going in flight. Flame spouted from the houses. The active King ravaged Uist with fire. The King made red the sword of battle. The farmers lost life and wealth.

The diminisher of the battle-gosling's hunger caused Skye to be plundered: the glad wolf reddened tooth in many a mortal wound upon Tiree. The Scots-expeller went mightily; the people of Mull ran to exhaustion. Greenland's King caused maids to weep, south in the islands.

Wide bore the active King his shields upon the level sand island; there was smoke from Islay when the King's men stirred up the burning. The sons of men south in Kintyre bowed beneath the swords' edges. The valiant battle-quickener then planned the Manxmen's fall.

Magnus himself is presented as a heroic figure, though not above a little chicanery and deception to further his cause. In AD1093 he came to terms with King Malcolm of Scotland, under which Magnus was allowed to claim 'all the islands off the west coast which were separated by water navigable by a ship with the rudder set'. In order to gain Kintyre, which was one of the richest and most fertile areas coveted by the Norse, Magnus 'had a skiff hauled across the narrow neck of land at Tarbert, with himself at the helm, and this is how he won the whole peninsula'. The story is told in the *Orkneyinga Saga*.

Magnus took his nickname 'Barelegs' from his adoption of the local style of dress; a kind of knee-length quilted tunic worn as war-dress. Something very similar can be seen on the later medieval carved grave-slabs. It was probably not anything like the kilt as we know it, for which there is a good case for saying that it was 'invented' for the visit of George IV to Edinburgh in 1822. Allowing for hyperbole, his personal appearance was apparently quite striking. He is described in Snorro Sturlason's *Magnus Saga*:

> King Magnus wore on his head a helmet, and carried on his arm a red shield, emblazoned with a golden lion; in his belt was a sword of exceeding sharpness, the hilt of which was ivory, enwreathed with inlaid gold; in his hand was a javelin; and over his coat of mail fell a short silken tunic of ruby colour, embroidered with a lion of auric hue; – and all acknowledged that none could surpass him in dignity and beauty.

SOMERLED

The saga extracts give some idea of the formidable nature of the occupying forces, but after a guerrilla campaign lasting several years, the Gaelic war leader Somerled defeated the Norse king of the Western Isles in a sea battle off the coast of Islay in 1156 or thereabouts, although Norse *sovereignty* was to last until the transfer achieved under the terms of the Treaty of Perth, in 1266.

Somerled was the son of a Norse mofher and a Scots (ie Gaelic-speaking) father. His Norse name *Sumarlidi* means 'summer traveller', referring to the time of year when Vikings did what Vikings do best – raiding, pillaging, raping, killing and looting. His name was anglicised as *Sorley*, which is how the Gaelic version *Somhairle* was pronounced. The name is still found in Gaeldom today: there is a Somerled Square in Portree, in Skye, while Scotland's greatest living poet, writing in both Gaelic and English, is Sorley Maclean. Somerled's influence on the history of Argyll and the Hebrides was to last for four hundred years and beyond.

Although his origins and ancestry are not well documented, clan tradition is definite in asserting that Somerled was descended from the kings of Dalriada, who established themselves before AD500 in what came to be known as Argyll. The descendants of Fergus Mor Mac Erc took control of a wide area of the mainland and islands of south-west Scotland.

Somerled was no less than the liberator of the Gaels from Norse rule, a twelfth century guerrilla leader whose exploits became legendary. No contemporary accounts have survived, but various clan histories give accounts of his campaigns. He first appears on the scene in the mountains of Ardgour and Morvern, where he and his father Gille-Bride with a few followers sought refuge from the Norse in the last area of the west coast not under their direct control. For the Norse were everywhere. From the Isle of Man in the south to the Orkney and Shetland islands in the north, they controlled everything, including large areas of the mainland. On the west coast they raided from Kintyre to Cape Wrath, while on the east coast they settled extensively in Caithness and as far south as the Beauly Firth, where the town of Dingwall shows from its name that it was once a Norse administrative centre, where a 'Thing' or 'parliament' once met.

According to clan historians and local traditions, Somerled was fishing for salmon near Lochaline when he was approached by some of the local people, named as MacInneses, with a view to leading them against Norse raiding parties who were in the area. He landed a fine fish, regarded as a good omen, which he then said he would give to his old father, hiding in a cave on the shores of Loch Linnhe, ten miles away. Somerled agreed to lead an attack against the Norse, and arranged a muster for the following day. A foretaste of his military cunning lay in his instructions to light a large number of camp fires that night, to confuse the opposition into thinking that they were to face a large force.

The next day, Somerled saw that his small band were outnumbered by the Norse party, so he ordered a herd of cattle nearby to be killed and skinned. Then his men marched round the hill above the Norsemen, first in their own clothes, then wearing the cow-skins with the hair turned outwards, then with the hair turned inwards. The Norse supposedly panicked at the sight of what they thought was a superior force, and prepared to evacuate. In the confusion, Somerled and his men attacked, killing large numbers.

These events probably took place in the 1130s. What seems to have happened is that Somerled continued these tactics throughout that decade, harrying the Norse whenever he could, taking advantage of his intimate knowledge of the complicated topography to stage quick raids on isolated Norse settlements before fading away into the mountain fastnesses. This was in a period when Norse power was on the wane, and the Norse settlers could no longer call on central authority to mount punitive expeditions; they had to fend for themselves.

The nearest Norse ruler with any military clout at his disposal was Olaf, 'king' of the Isle of Man. Soon after 1140, by which time Somerled controlled the lands of Lorn, mid-Argyll, Kintyre and Knapdale, Olaf mounted a naval expedition to quell an uprising in the northern Hebrides. On his way north he camped near Ardnamurchan Point, where Somerled caught up with him.

Now Olaf had a daughter Ragnhilda, whom Somerled resolved to marry. Diplomatically this would have been tantamount to handing over all Olaf's territories to Somerled and his line, and Olaf refused outright. But now Somerled brought his Special Forces unit into play. He had a close friend, Maurice MacNeill, who was one of the crew in Olaf's galley, a shipwright. Under cover of darkness, he slipped into the water beside Olaf's longship, and bored holes in the hull below the waterline, filling the holes with a mixture of tallow and butter.

In the sheltered waters of an inshore anchorage, nothing happened, but next day, when Olaf's fleet was rounding the turbulent waters of Ardnamurchan Point, the tallow and butter filling was dislodged by the action of the waves, and Olaf's galley began to sink. Somerled of course was on hand to effect a rescue, but demanded a promise of the king's daughter in marriage first. Under the circumstances, Olaf was compelled to agree! The holes in his ship were filled with pins specially prepared by Maurice, and Somerled had proved once again that campaigns are not only won by full-scale pitched battles.

From that day, Maurice's descendants took the name MacIntyre, which in Gaelic means 'son of the carpenter' (mac an-t'saoir), and all of today's MacIntyres would like to think they are descended from this man.

Somerled was now able to establish a headquarters on the island of Islay. His military citadel was the fortress of Dunivaig, on the south-east coast, but his political and administrative headquarters was at Finlaggan. There today two small islands in Loch Finlaggan bear the traces of the buildings erected by Somerled and his successors.

In 1153 King David I of Scotland died. He was a powerful, able and influential ruler. He was succeeded by his grandson Malcolm IV, a weak and feeble youth, nicknamed Malcolm the Maiden. Somerled took the opportunity to consolidate his mainland holdings, to which, unlike his island dominions, he had no claim through his Norse connections. Perhaps he felt he had to move quickly to fill the power vacuum left in the west by David's death, before the Norse moved in. He was in a state of rebellion against the Scottish King until 1159; two royal charters of 1160 were dated 'on the next Christmas after the reconcilement of the King and Somerled'.

Meanwhile, a rebellion had broken out on the Isle of Man. King Olaf was killed by his nephews, who in turn were seized and killed by Olaf's son, Godfrey (Godred). Somerled now became involved in the fate of his late father-in-law's kingdom, and installed his own son Dugald as ruler. Godfrey sailed to do battle with Somerled, and a great naval battle took place off the west coast of Islay on Epiphany, 6 January 1156. Godfrey suffered great losses, but so did Somerled, and he was unable to follow up his advantage.

According to clan tradition, Somerled's success on this occasion was due to the fact that, whereas Godfrey was equipped with the superb ocean-going longships we associate with the Vikings, Somerled used the smaller, more manoevrable Hebridean galley, the *nyvaigs* or 'little ships' which some claim gave their name to Dunivaig itself – the fort of the little ships. The main difference between the two types of craft was in the steering mechanism. The longships or *biorlinns* were steered by means of a long steering oar on the right-hand (or 'starboard') side of the ship, attached to a tiller which passed across the stern. Somerled either invented, or was the first to apply widely, the principle of a hinged rudder, which gave vastly increased manoevrability. This ship is often depicted on the late medieval carved grave-slabs prepared under the patronage of Somerled's successors between 1350 and 1500.

Godfrey and Somerled agreed terms, dividing the remnants of the Norse kingdom between them, but two years later Somerled invaded the Isle of Man with fifty-three ships. Godfrey fled to Norway. Somerled took the title *Ri Innse Gall & Cind tire* – ruler of the Islands of the Strangers (the Hebrides) and Kintyre. In Latin he was called *Rex Insularum* – King of the Isles.

Such designations did not endear him to the Scottish state and in 1164 Somerled once more found himself at odds with Malcolm IV. Somerled sailed up the Clyde with a fleet of 160 galleys, and set up camp near Paisley. Whát happened next is a matter of some dispute. 'Official' Scottish sources talk of a great battle, in which Somerled was defeated and killed;

MacDonald clan histories talk of treachery and assassination. The MacDonald account is more detailed, and on balance, more probable. According to it, Somerled was killed by his sister's son, who was bribed by Malcolm's advisers. He was able to gain access to Somerled's tent at night, because of his kinship, where he stabbed his uncle and made good his escape. This took place near Renfrew, on what is now the site of Glasgow Airport. When the death of their war-leader was discovered, the Gaels decamped and went home. It is said that Somerled was buried at Saddell, on the east coast of Kintyre.

It is impossible to overstate Somerled's importance in the history of the Western Isles. After his death his lands were divided between his two surviving sons, Dugall and Reginald. Dugall (from whom all MacDougalls are descended) inherited Lorn, Benderloch, Lismore, the Garvellachs and the Treshnish islands, Mull, Coll, Tiree and the north end of Jura. Reginald got everything else, and on his death his holdings were divided between his sons Donald and Ruari. Ruari got 'Garmoran' (Moidart, Arisaig, Morar and Knoydart), Eigg, Rum, Barra and Uist, while Donald inherited Islay, Colonsay, Oronsay, Kintyre, Ardnamurchan, Morvern and the south end of Jura. It is this Donald who is the progenitor of Clan Donald, and through him all MacDonalds trace their descent from Somerled and ultimately from the kings of Dalriada and the High Kings of Ireland.

THE LORDS OF THE ISLES

Little is known of Reginald. Known in Latin as *Reginaldus*, his Norse name was *Rognvaldr*, translated into Gaelic as *Raghnall*, anglicised as *Ranald*. It is thought that Saddell Abbey was founded by Somerled in 1160, but it was certainly completed under Reginald's supervision. He is supposed to have been a very religious man. Tradition has it that he undertook a pilgrimage to Rome, and that he brought back some earth from there which he scattered on the site of

95

Saddell Abbey. He died in 1207 and is thought to have been buried at Iona.

Little is known of Reginald's son Donald, despite his importance as the 'founder' of Clan Donald. He died at Shipness in 1249 and was buried at Iona. In 1266, during the time of his son Angus Mor (Big Angus), the legal status of the Lords of the Isles changed, for under the Treaty of Perth all Norse possessions in the Western Isles were ceded to the King of Scotland. In 1263 King Haakon of Norway had made one last attempt to reassert Norse control of the Western Isles, and had brought his fleet of galleys right up the Firth of Clyde, to have a final showdown with the Scots. 'Terror was caused by the leader of mighty deeds of gaping-beaked ships, about the lands that are washed with the drizzling rain of western storms.' Angus Mor was forced to give in to Haakon's superior force; really he had no choice. His island lands were legally under Haakon's sovereignty. During the late summer and autumn of 1263 Haakon's galleys anchored in Lamlash Bay, while the land troops of Alexander III were encamped on the mainland opposite, near Ayr. Dominican monks tried to negotiate terms between the two kings. Losing patience, Haakon sent Angus Mor and Dugall MacRuairi up Loch Long on a raid designed to show the Scottish king that he could strike at the very heart of his lands. For the galleys were pulled across the narrow isthmus at Tarbet onto Loch Lomond, from where they raided far into Lennox and the Stirling plain.

But in the end it was the weather which was Haakon's undoing. Not drizzling rain, but a mighty storm was unleashed on the Norwegian fleet, anchored off the Cumbraes, on 1 October 1263. Some longships were driven ashore on the Clyde coast near Largs, where they came under attack from Alexander's armies. Haakon landed some reinforcements, there was a brief skirmish, and next day the Norse withdrew, after burying their dead and burning the wrecked longships. That was the Battle of Largs.

Haakon sailed for home, but died on the way, at Kirkwall

in the Orkneys. His successor Magnus agreed to the Treaty of Perth in 1266, under which the former Norwegian territories in the Hebrides were purchased for the sum of 4,000 silver marks and an annual payment of 100 marks in perpetuity, and formally ceded to the Scottish crown. To seal the bargain, Alexander's daughter Margaret was married to Eric, the heir to the Norwegian throne. Margaret became Queen of Norway, but died in childbirth in 1283. But when Alexander III died as the result of a riding accident in 1286 without a male heir, his infant grand-daughter Margaret, the 'Maid of Norway', was recognised as the heir to the Scottish throne. But her death, in Orkney, on her way to Edinburgh in 1290 precipitated the constitutional crisis which resulted in the Wars of Independence and ultimately in the flourishing of Clan Donald.

Angus Mor died around 1292, but *his* son Angus Og (Wee Angus) came to prominence during Scotland's Wars of Independence in the early fourteenth century. Angus Og fought alongside Robert the Bruce at the Battle of Bannockburn in 1314, leading men from Kintyre and Islay, and who knows, perhaps also men from other islands under his control, of which Colonsay was one. Today his name is well known in Scotland, though more from a cartoon character in a Scottish tabloid newspaper than as the Celtic hero who helped free Scotland from English control. After Bannockburn, a grateful king bestowed his thanks on Angus Og. By contrast, the descendants of Dugall backed the losing side in the Wars of Independence, and lost everything.

Saddell Abbey was completed by about 1205. Now in ruins, having been quarried in the eighteenth century for the farm buildings around Saddell Castle, little now remains to indicate its former importance. In founding an abbey there, and importing a community of Cistercian monks from Mellifont in Ireland to run it, Somerled and Reginald were creating a symbol of their power, indicating to the Scottish kings that they were rulers of equal stature, at a time when monasteries and abbeys were going up all over Scotland under the patronage of David I. They were symbolically thumbing their noses at the Kings of Scotland, who looked to their Anglo-Norman cousins in England for their religious inspiration, when it came to founding abbeys and monasteries. Thus, the other ten Cistercian monasteries in Scotland owed their existence to the abbey of Rievaulx, in Yorkshire, or to its major Scottish monastic colony, Melrose. By placing an abbey on the east side of Kintyre, within sight of the Ayrshire coast, Somerled was almost flaunting his position as *Rex Insularum*. Small wonder that Malcolm IV and his Stewart aides found it necessary to diminish Somerled's power at almost any cost.

Starting with Reginald, the descendants of Somerled and the Lords of the Isles who carried on his lineage in the fourteenth century, made grants of lands to Saddell Abbey to ensure its success. This began a long period of patronage, from which several other religious foundations in Argyll benefitted, including the Benedictine abbey at Iona, the Valliscaulian priory at Ardchattan, and most importantly for visitors to Colonsay and Oronsay, the Augustinian priory on Oronsay.

Any understanding of Oronsay Priory and its importance is impossible without an understanding of the Lordship of the Isles. The first to assume the title was John (Iain) of Islay, son of Angus Og, grandson of Donald, the grandson of Somerled. Under his patronage, the great parish church at Killean, on the west coast of Kintyre, was established, many smaller stone chapels and churches were erected, more lands were given to Saddell Abbey, schools of sculpture were founded and financed at Iona, Oronsay, Kilmartin and Saddell, and the Augustinian Priory at Oronsay was built.

It is an impressive record, which was paralleled on the political front. From his headquarters at Finlaggan the first Lord of the Isles ruled his dominions – he was the first to use the title *Dominus Insularum* (rather than *Rex Insularum*), possibly out of deference to his father-in-law, who was the heir of the Stewart kings of Scotland. John was Lord of the

Isles from 1336 to 1387. His first marriage to Amie MacRuari united the lineages of Reginald's sons Donald and Dugall; his second marriage was to Margaret Stewart, daughter of Robert Stewart who became Robert II of Scotland in 1371.

John's son Donald was the second Lord of the Isles, from 1387 to 1423. He married Mary Leslie, the heiress to the Earldom of Ross, and it was he who led islanders into battle at Harlaw in 1411.

The third Lord of the Isles was Alexander (Gaelic: Alasdair), the son of Donald of Harlaw. He ruled from 1423 to 1449 and had a colourful career. Captured by James I in 1428 and imprisoned in Tantallon Castle, he was later released and defeated the royal army in battle in 1431. Subsequently he made peace with the king and was recognised as Earl of Ross and appointed Royal Justiciar for Scotland north of the River Forth. He died at Dingwall and was buried at the cathedral in Fortrose in Easter Ross.

The fourth and last Lord of the Isles was another John, the son of Alexander. Born in 1434, he ran the Lordship from 1449 to 1493. He quarrelled continually with his wife, his son and the king. In 1462 he was lured into a treaty with the English King Edward IV, the Treaty of Ardtornish-Westminster. Some money changed hands, but the complicated plans, involving co-ordinating an invasion of Lowland Scotland with simultaneous thrusts from John in the west and the Earl of Douglas in the Borders, were never likely to succeed. In 1464 a truce was agreed between England and Scotland, and when commissioners from Scotland were invited to England in 1475 to negotiate a permanent treaty, the 1462 Treaty between John, Lord of the Isles and Edward, King of England, came to light.

John was summoned to appear before the Scottish Parliament in Edinburgh, and all his lands and estates were forfeited. But his contrition was so convincing that in 1476 the King pardoned him, restoring his island domains, but not the Earldom of Ross or the lands of Kintyre and Knapdale. But the respite was temporary. In 1490 John's son and heir Angus was murdered at Inverness, while plotting apparently to re-take Ross. In 1491 John's nephew Alexander of Lochalsh took over the struggle, but he too was killed. In 1493, James IV lost patience and once again all the lands of the Lordship were forfeited, this time for ever. The last Lord of the Isles died at Dundee in 1503, living in lodgings on a small state pension. He was probably buried in Paisley Abbey.

The Lords of the Isles brought pride and prestige to an embattled minority in a remote region. Ultimately, they were too powerful and too successful, and posed a threat to the Scottish state which its kings could not allow to go unchallenged. The title itself did not end with the forfeiture of 1493. Inalienably annexed to the Crown in 1542, it is now held by HRH the Prince of Wales and Earl of Chester, Duke of Cornwall and Duke of Rothesay, Earl of Carrick and Baron Renfrew, Lord of the Isles and Great Steward of Scotland – the current heir to the throne, in whose veins the blood of Somerled, admittedly much diluted, flows.

It is worth reflecting on the fact that the final forfeiture of the Lordship of the Isles took place in the year after Christopher Columbus discovered America, the continent that would one day become the new home for thousands of Gaels displaced by the social chaos which accompanied the breakup of the Lordship and the imposition of the rule of Scots law on the western frontier of the Scottish state.

DONALD DUBH

The forfeiture of 1493 was not quite the end of the story. Donald Dubh (Black Donald), the son of Angus who was killed at Inverness in 1490, was born at the Campbell stronghold of Innis Chonnell on Loch Awe after his father's death. After the forfeiture he was held in captivity there, but was rescued by the MacDonalds of Glencoe in 1501. After three campaigns by government forces he was recaptured in 1506 and imprisoned in Edinburgh Castle. He escaped from there in 1544 and was recognised as Lord of the Isles by all the branches of Clan Donald, and by many other clan chieftains. At Knockfergus, in Ireland, he assembled a force of 180 galleys and 4,000 fighting men, but while organising an invasion of Scotland he died at Drogheda of a sudden fever at the end of 1545; the rebellion then collapsed.

THE COUNCIL OF THE ISLES

Donald Monro, the Dean of the Isles, writing in 1549 presumably as the result of interviewing eyewitnesses to the way Donald Dubh's regime was conducted, gives a little information about the make-up of the Council of the Isles. According to Dean Monro, the Council was made up of fourteen members who:

> sat down into the Counsell-Ile, and decernit, decreitit and gave suits furth upon all debaitable matters according to the Laws made be Renald McSomharkle [ie, Reginald, son of Somerled] callit in his time King of the Occident Iles, and albeit thair Lord were at his hunting or at ony other games, yet thai sate every ane at thair Counsell ministring justice. In thair time thair was great peace and welth in the Iles throw the ministration of justice.

However, our main source for the way things were done comes from Hugh MacDonald of Sleat, whose manuscript account compiled during the seventeenth century has survived. He too describes the Council, supplying details which must have been passed on by word of mouth for hundreds of years:

> There was a table of stone where this council sat in the Island of Finlaggan; the which table, with the stone on which Macdonald sat, was carried away by Argyle with the bells that were at Icolmkill [Iona]. Moreover, there was a judge in every Isle for the discussion of all controversies, who had lands from Macdonald for their trouble,

and likewise the eleventh part of every action decided, but there might still be an appeal to the council of the Isles. Macfinnon was obliged to see weights and measures adjusted; and Macduffie, or MacFie of Colonsay, kept the records of the Isles.

At last, a Colonsay connection! What happened to the records kept by the MacDuffies of Colonsay, we do not know. It is presumed that they were destroyed by Argyll, along with the stone table and MacDonald's stone seat. At least, they do not appear to be amongst the archives surviving at Inverary Castle, and they are not in Islay or Colonsay, or in any national collections, so regretfully it must be concluded that the evidence for much of what is known about the Lordship must be fragmentary.

Many charters and papers issued by the Lords of the Isles do survive, but usually because they were written in Dingwall, Inverness, Ardtornish, Aros, Perth, or any of about thirty other places scattered around Ross-shire and the Western Isles. For although Finlaggan was the centre of the Lordship, the place where the Council met and where inauguration ceremonies were carried out, the Lord of the Isles was constantly on the move, circulating round his territories, issuing charters and instructions.

The Lord of the Isles and his entourage must have visited Colonsay and Oronsay many times but, despite the MacDuffie connection, only two records have survived. A charter in the name of 'Alexander de Insulis de Lochalch' with the consent of the Council granting lands in Lochalsh to Ewen Cameron, was issued at Colonsay ('Collinsay' in the original Latin text) on 29 July 1492. Then on 1 August 1492 a charter was issued from Oronsay ('Orwinsai') by John, Lord of the Isles and Alexander of the Isles, Lord of Lochalsh, with the consent of their Council, granting half of the office of bailie of the island of Tiree to John MacLean of Lochbuie. We know the names of some of the people who accompanied the Lord of the Isles to Colonsay and Oronsay in 1492, because their signatures appear on the two charters as witnesses: Roderick MacLeod, son of Alexander MacLeod of Glenelg, Colinus Nigelli Gewa (Malcolm MacNeill of Gigha), Angus Martin (or MacMartin), possibly from Letterfinlay beside Loch Lochy, Duncan Martin, possibly the brother of Angus, John Duff, son of Duncan, John MacKinnon, the abbot of Iona, John MacIan of Ardnamurchan, and Roderick MacLeod of Lewis. The geographical range of these witnesses gives some idea of the degree of organisation that must have been required when the Lord of the Isles and his Council were on one of their periodic peregrinations.

After this whirlwind review of the history of the Lords of the Isles, the stage is now set to explore the ways in which Colonsay and Oronsay were affected by these events.

6 MacDONALDS AND MacDUFFIES

During the period of the Lordship of the Isles, Colonsay and Oronsay were an important feature of the political and religious Hebridean landscape, due in large measure to the magnificent Augustinian priory on Oronsay.

ORONSAY PRIORY

The priory nestles under the rocky cliffs of Beinn Oronsay. According to tradition, the spot was chosen because of its association with St Columba though, as we have seen, there is no real historical evidence for this. But the church dedication is to St Columba, and the story persists that Columba landed in Oronsay in AD563. If he did, it must have been in clear weather, for it is said that he climbed to the summit of Beinn Oronsay, could still see the coastline of Ireland, and so resumed the journey that was to take him to Iona. Exactly 1,350 years later, in the year before the outbreak of World War I, another great leader stood on the same lofty spot in his capacity as First Lord of the Admiralty, viewing the 3rd Battle Squadron of the Royal Navy at gunnery practice. With his sense of history, it is certain that Winston Churchill appreciated the association.

The ruins of the priory, which was founded sometime between 1330 and 1350, are impressive, though only the so-called 'Prior's House' is roofed, everything else being open to the sky. But enough remains of the cloisters and the surrounding buildings to reconstruct in the mind's eye something of what the community would have looked like in the fourteenth century. In its original condition it would have looked very much like the abbey at Iona, which today has been largely restored thanks to the efforts of the Iona Community. In size and importance these two establishments would have seemed comparable in their heyday.

Certainly compared to the mainland sites of Ardchattan and Saddell, both now very ruinous, there is a lot more to see at Oronsay. The present church building lies at the south side of the square of buildings, although there is clear architectural evidence that in the earliest phase of construction it was on the north. At the eastern end of the church stands the high altar, dating probably from the late fifteenth century. The square annexe at the west end of the sanctuary may have been intended as the base of a tower.

Off the south wall of the church is a small chapel enclosure known as the MacDuffie Aisle. Here the hereditary MacDuffie priors and chiefs were buried. Their surviving gravestones have been removed to the Prior's House, the roofed building on the north side of the complex, along with other elaborately carved stones that were displayed inside the church in the nineteenth century.

The north side of the square, part of which was originally the church building, was used later as a refectory – the place where the community met together to eat and drink.

The easterly range of buildings formed the accommodation quarters, store houses and workshops of the religious community. This area appears to have been remodelled several times. Around 1800 it was subdivided to create a burial place for the McNeills of Colonsay, and several interesting gravestones survive there today. The crest of the McNeills of Colonsay can be seen above a doorway. One of the stones commemorates Major-General Sir John Carstairs McNeill, who died in 1904. Another was erected in 1891, in memory of Margaret Ferooza McNeill, by her children.

Thomas Pennant has provided us with views of the priory

in 1772, from which the original appearance of much of the buildings can be deduced. Parts of the remaining cloister were apparently reconstructed in 1883. Two of the pier-slabs holding up the cloister arches were seen by Pennant in 1772 and have been incorporated into the restoration. From the inscriptions on these slabs it can be deduced that the cloisters were remodelled shortly before 1500. One reads CELESTINUS CANONICUS GUBERNATOR HUIUS OPERIS ('Canon Celestinus, director of this work'); and the other says MAELSEACHLAIND SAER OCUIND FECIT ISTUD OPUS ('Mael-Sechlainn O Cuinn, mason, made this work'). The style of the lettering, known as black-letter, indicates a date of just before 1500.

The two individuals mentioned in these inscriptions turn up in other parts of the priory. The grave-slab of Canon Celestinus is in the Prior's House. Celestinus is the usual Latin form of the Gaelic name *Gill-easbuig*, meaning 'servant of the bishop'. The modern form is Gillespie. Interestingly, the style of the lettering on his gravestone is not black-letter but Lombardic capitals – just at this time the transition from one to the other was taking place in the West Highlands.

The mason Mael-Sechlainn O Cuinn was also the sculptor who carved the famous Oronsay Cross, which stands in its original position near the south-west corner of the priory church. An inscription on the pedestal says: MAELSEACHLAIND SAER OCUINN FECIT ISTAM CRUCEM ('Mael-Sechlainn O Cuinn, mason, made this cross').

The Oronsay Cross is one of the finest monuments of its kind in Scotland, comparable with the cross at Kilchoman in Islay, and second only to the superlative Campbeltown Cross. From the style of carving we know that the mason was trained at the Iona workshop, under the patronage of the Lords of the Isles. Both sides are carved; the front has an unusually unmutilated crucifixion. Near the bottom of the front of the cross is an inscription: HEC EST CRUX COLINI FILII CRISTINI MEICDUFACI ('This is the cross of Colinus, son of Cristinus MacDuffie').

From this we can deduce that Colinus MacDuffie was chief

of his clan around 1500. Colinus is the Latin for Malcolm, in Gaelic *Gille-Coluim*, the servant of Colum (Columba). As already noted, the dedication of the priory church is to St Columba.

MACDUFFIES

The origin of the MacDuffie name is interesting and has given rise to much speculation. In Gaelic *dub-shide or dubh-sithe* means 'the black peace', so MacDuffie can be translated as 'son of the black peace'. It has been suggested that this may refer to the dark robes worn by monks, but as the Gaelic word *sithe* (pronounced 'shee') can also mean 'magical' or 'supernatural', the MacDuffie name could equally well have to do with 'black magic'. The word has even found its way into English in 'banshee', from the Gaelic *bean-sithe*, the female fairy whose wailing and shrieking foretold the approaching death of a member of a family. It is by no means beyond the bounds of possibility that the hereditary MacDuffie priors of Oronsay had their ancestral roots in the remote pre-Christian past, as hereditary priests in the Iron Age or earlier. But of course, this must remain a matter of speculation.

In Islay and Jura the surname Shaw is thought to derive from *sithe*, and as we shall see, there are in fact many links between Islay, Jura and Colonsay and the MacDuffies. And of course all McFees, McPhees, Duffys and all the myriad variations also derive from the MacDuffies. If these derivations seem excessively tortuous, spare a thought for the Curries who derive from the bardic family of MacMhuirich (in the genitive case, the 'mh' is silent!).

There are other stones in Oronsay with inscriptions relevant to the MacDuffies and, as most are now almost totally illegible, it is perhaps worthwhile to mention them here.

The grave-slab of Malcolm MacDuffie's wife, Mariota, is in the Prior's House. It is broken in two, and very worn. It depicts a laywoman standing below a triple canopy, with an angel at each side supporting the pillow on which her head rests. She has an elaborate hair-do and head-dress, described as 'caul-like' by the Royal Commission. She wears a long, full-sleeved robe and a cloak with a large circular fastening (a brooch?) at the neck. She is holding a rosary and a bible. Two dogs nestle in her lap. On the lower half of the slab are two other female figures, and right at the bottom, a galley in full sail, surrounded by fish and other small creatures.

Mariota was the daughter of Alexander, the son of John MacIan of Ardnamurchan. There were close ties between the MacIans and the MacDuffies over many generations. Mariota commissioned a grave-slab for her brother John MacIan of Ardnamurchan, who is buried at Iona. On the inscription of that stone, we are told that 'Mariota MacIan, his sister, wife of Malcolmus MacDuffie, lord of Dunevin in Colonsay, bought this stone for her brother'. She may have bought a slab for herself at the same time. The 'Dunevin' of the Iona description is of course the very same Dùn Éibhinn, encountered as an Iron Age fort in chapter 4. It is very likely that some of the surviving remains inside the fort date from the Middle Ages, and were occupied by the MacDuffies at that time. So for anybody interested in soaking up some of the medieval ambience of their MacDuffie ancestry, a visit to the fort behind Scalasaig, and of course to Oronsay, is strongly recommended.

IAIN A'CHUAIN

An extraordinary story surrounds one of Mariota's children, named John. It was a common custom in those days for ruling families to exchange children, who were fostered out until they were old enough to return to reclaim their birthright. One purpose behind this custom may have been to minimise clan feuding by building up personal contacts between neighbours. Apparently the MacDuffies at 'Dunevin' agreed to exchange sons with the MacNeills of Barra. The MacNeill wife, the birth of her baby imminent, set out in an open boat from Barra to sail to Colonsay, intending to give birth there.

But the baby was born on the way. To safeguard the mother and baby from the elements, the crew of her boat had the idea of killing a cow which they were carrying. They wrapped the mother and child in the warm carcase, and delivered them safely to Colonsay. The child was known thereafter as Iain a'Chuain – John of the Ocean. Some of the MacNeills of Colonsay claim descent from him, saying that he stayed on Colonsay as an adult.

EARLY RECORDS

Records of the earlier MacDuffies are rather scanty. The first recorded usage of the name is in 1164, when a deputation from Iona went to Derry to ask the abbot there to take charge of Iona, seeking liberation from the by then ineffective ecclesiastical control of Norway. A manuscript of 1467, which includes genealogical compilation thought to have been made around 1400, gives little more than a list of names of MacDuffies. The final generation listed were Donald, Niall and Gille-Coluim, the three sons of Gill-easbuig. Donald MacDuffie, thought to be the older brother of Malcolm of the Oronsay Cross, witnessed a charter at Dingwall for John, first Lord of the Isles, in April 1463, while in November 1472, presumably still the chief of his clan, he witnessed a charter at Inverlochy for Celestinus, Lord of Lochalsh. Malcolm MacDuffie was Donald's brother. It is not known when he succeeded as chief.

In 1506, according to the Exchequer Rolls of Scotland, Colonsay was 'let to Archibald MacEachan for Malcolm MacDuffie'. The Latin text has '. . .*assedatur Archibaldo McCachan ex parte Malcolmi Makcofee*' – yet another version of the name: Malcolm MacDuffie held Colonsay on behalf of the Crown, and his brother-in-law, John MacIan of Ardnamurchan, went surety for the rental transactions into which he entered at the time. Yet in 1509, John MacIan was claiming Colonsay for himself, on the grounds that it had been granted to him by the Earl of Lennox. It can be assumed that Malcolm MacDuffie must have died shortly before.

It has been suggested that by putting forward this claim, John MacIan was safeguarding the interests of a young nephew. Certainly there are no more MacDuffies in the records until 1531, when Morphe Makphe of Colonsay was summoned to appear before parliament to face charges of treason, arising out of his participation, along with other island chiefs, in the uprising headed by Alexander MacDonald of Islay. Morphe is the normal Scotticised form of the Gaelic name *Murchad* (now Murdoch), and indeed, we find the tombstone of Murchadh MacDuffie of Colonsay in the Prior's House at Oronsay Priory. He died in 1539. His grave-slab is very ornate and is one of the finest products of the Oronsay School of carving. It shows a stag and two hinds pursued by deer-hounds. Down the middle of the stone is a large claymore sword in its scabbard, surrounded by elaborate foliage. At the bottom of the stone is a finely carved galley in full sail, the prow, hinged rudder and rigging clearly visible.

Murchadh (Murdoch) was succeeded by John Mael MacIan McFee of Colonsay, pardoned in 1546, along with his brother Angus, for his part in the burning of the Ayrshire town of Saltcoats. He was succeeded by his cousin Murdoch, son of the Murchardus MacDuffie of Colonsay who died in 1539. He is very likely the chief met by Donald Munro, Dean of the Isles, when he toured the Hebrides in 1549. Dean Munro says: 'Colonsay is brukit [possessed] by ane gentle capitane called McDuffyhe'.

Murchadh's son Donald was chief from about 1593 to about 1609. It was he who signed the Statutes of Icolmkill (Iona) on behalf of the MacDuffies. This was an attempt by James VI to restore order and impose the rule of law, using the authority of the church to bolster his political weakness. He was succeeded by his brother Malcolm, destined to be the last chief of his clan. His story, and the circumstances surrounding his murder in 1623, will be told in chapter 7.

ORONSAY PRIORS

We know a little about some of the priors of Oronsay from other grave-slabs. Papal archives supply the name of Maurice Brichi (Muireach, son of Gille-Brigde). He was the son of a canon regular and, judging from his name, a member of the MacMhuirich family. He was prior of Oronsay from about 1362 to 1397. His son Donald succeeded him and was prior until 1426. Some time after 1500 a Canon Bricius (ie Gille-Brigde) MacMhuirich was buried at Oronsay, and his gravestone survives.

Canon MacMhuirich is depicted on his stone in a low-relief effigy, dressed as an Augustinian canon in choir vestments. The detail of his ecclesiastical outfit is still clear and sharp, after nearly five hundred years.

Dating possibly from around 1550, another slab commemorates Canon Bricius MacDuffie and Canon Patricius his father. Most of the stone is taken up with a sword and interlaced foliage, rather inappropriate one would have thought. However, careful examination of the slab shows that the small figure of the canon at the top of the stone has been added later, very likely to a stone held in stock at the Oronsay workshops.

In the 1530s the prior was Donald MacPhail. In April 1538 Donald MacDuffie was appointed prior by papal authority, and his gravestone survives. He was undoubtedly related to the Murdoch MacDuffie who became chief in 1549. Donald MacDuffie died before 1555, when Donald Lamont took over. Donald MacDuffie's stone is another very detailed effigy, showing his tonsured head resting on a pillow, though from the canopy over his head and the disposition of his garments he is also shown standing. His right hand is raised in blessing and in his left hand he holds a finely carved pastoral staff. The detail of his vestments is very clear.

Of the other stones at Oronsay, two effigies of men in

111

armour may well be other MacDuffie chiefs, though there are no identifying inscriptions. The sharp detail gives a good idea of what the chiefs would have looked like, in the fifteenth century. Many of the other stones – there are thirty in all – also display interesting features.

Scratched on the pedestal of the Oronsay Cross is a clue to the meaning of what was happening there, from the foundation of the priory around 1350 until the Protestant Reformation. At the south-east corner of the socket-stone is the worn dial of a 'mass-clock', a circle 0.28m (11in) in diameter divided into 24 segments. In the centre a fragment of the original metal gnomon can still be seen. Apart from the political symbolism of a monastic community functioning under the patronage of the Lords of the Isles, the religious significance of this place was that here the power of the Christian religion to maintain the celebration of *its* mysteries literally round the clock, on every day of the year, was made manifest. And not just here, but at Ardchattan, Saddell and Iona, as well as at the numerous communities more obviously under the territorial control of the Scottish state, the daily round of worship continued, uninterrupted, for at least two hundred and ten years.

MEDIEVAL CHURCHES

While Oronsay Priory was a major regional religious centre, it did not function as the working church for the inhabitants of Colonsay and Oronsay. This role was fulfilled by the parish church, which was located at Lower Kilchattan, in the middle of Colonsay near the western shore. Since the dedication is to St Catán, there was very likely an Early Christian chapel there, but the surviving remains date from the late fourteenth century. There are no early grave-slabs or stones, either Early Christian or medieval. It lies just across the road from the Bronze Age standing stones at Drumclach (Fingal's Limpet Hammers).

The only other medieval church site on the islands is at

Teampull a'Ghlinne, on the road to Garvard. The ruins lie close to the road, and traditionally were used as a resting place for travellers and funeral processions waiting to cross the tidal flats to Oronsay. It also dates from the fourteenth century.

The impact of all this religious activity on the local inhabitants was, nevertheless, short-lived. Despite the appointment of another Malcolm MacDuffie as Commendator (lay prior) of Oronsay in 1561, the new Protestant religion had little support in the islands, throughout the seventeenth and eighteenth centuries.

SMUGGLERS AND PIRATES

This Malcolm MacDuffie, Commendator, was quite a rascal. He was involved in a court action in 1583 which gives, in dramatic language, some idea of the unpredictability of life in the wild West, still only ninety years after the forfeiture of the Lords of the Isles. An action was raised against Malcolm by William Somervell, a burgess of the town of Renfrew, along with two merchants, Norman Mackynnie and John Dikie. According to Somervell, he was in a 'bark' decked out for the purpose of a fishing expedition to 'Lochpewle', 'soberlie and singlie equippagit', according to his account in the legal records. Near Culdaff on the north coast of Ireland Somervell's boat was set upon by two boatloads of pirates – numbering fifty men, clearly as dastardly a group of ruffians as had ever been seen by this law-abiding merchant. One of the pirate ships belonged to Gillecallum Macforsum and it transpired that it was under charter to Malcolm MacDuffie of Colonsay!

What happened next sounds fairly gruesome. They boarded Somervell's ship 'and shot me the said William Somervell throu the arme with ane flwkit (fluked or barbed) arrow, and the said Normound throw the arme, alsua Johnne Chalmiris schot in at his face and out at his neck'. In spelling almost as colourful as the events described, Somervell goes on to relate how his son was 'straikin in at the mouth with ane suorde, Henry Fennesoun schot in the thie (thigh) with ane darte, Michaell Smyth schot throw the hand and metulat of his formest fingare, to the grite effusioun of the foirsaidis persounes blude in ane grite quantite'.

So far, it seemed like a fairly straightforward case of piracy. But in a fishing boat supposedly 'soberlie equippagit', what are we to make of the list of 'guidis and geir' taken by the ruffians: 7 puncheons of wine, 60 gallons of 'acquavitey' (whisky), 6lbs of salmon, 2 barrels of madder (a natural red dye) and 2 of alum, 12 pieces of ordnance, a quantity of powder and bullets, 17 one-handed and 2 two-handed swords, 1 doz. steel bonnets, 1 habergeon or coat of mail, 4 hogsheads of beer and 4 hogsheads of salt, besides all their clothing, to the total value of £666.13s.4d. (Scots).

It seems obvious that the merchants of Renfrew were on a gun-running and smuggling expedition to Ireland. When Malcolm MacDuffie appeared before the bailies, he denied all knowledge of the events, and in fact no evidence was forthcoming to connect him with the affair, apart from the admission that Macforsum's boat was under charter to him when he was summoned. So, no doubt reluctantly, 'the baillies absolvit the said Malcolme, and Gorrie MacFauld, his serueand, fra the complaneris bill and clame foirsaid for ewir'.

MACLEANS VS MACDONALDS

The particular squabble that was to affect Colonsay and Oronsay in the last years of the sixteenth century and the first two decades of the seventeenth was the disagreement between the MacDonalds of Islay and the Macleans of Duart in Mull over ownership of certain lands in the Rinns of Islay.

Angus MacDonald had succeeded to the chieftaincy of the major branch of Clan Donald in 1567, while Lachlan Maclean of Duart came of age in 1578. These two larger-than-life characters, and their followers and relations, were to keep their part of the Western Isles in turmoil and upheaval for the best part of fifty years.

In 1579 Angus MacDonald married Lachlan Maclean's sister, at the insistence of the government, and it was hoped that this imposed relationship would put an end to the quarrel. But on a visit to Duart Castle, Angus was taken prisoner and held there until he agreed to sign away his rights to the Rinns of Islay. On his release he had to leave his son James and his brother Ranald as hostages. Soon after, Lachlan arrived in Islay, with young James, to assert his claim to the Rinns. But Angus MacDonald neatly turned the tables, and Lachlan and eighty-six of his followers were arrested at a banquet in their honour. Back in Mull, one of Lachlan's kinsmen, Alan Maclean, saw his chance to assume the Maclean chieftancy. He let it be known that Ranald MacDonald, Angus's brother, had been put to death in revenge, hoping that the MacDonalds would take out their anger on the captive Macleans. His scheme very nearly worked. The eighty-seven Macleans were put to death at the rate of two a day, until only Lachlan was left alive. At the last minute news of Alan Maclean's deception leaked out. Lachlan's execution had been delayed only because Angus MacDonald had an accident on the way to witness his brother-in-law's end.

In a portent of some significance, James VI appointed various important members of Clan Campbell to act as mediators. In 1587 Angus MacDonald released Lachlan Maclean in a deal which involved the transfer of eight Maclean hostages to Islay. But the totally incorrigible Lachlan immediately raided Islay, while Angus raided Mull and Tiree in retaliation. While mustering his forces for another attack on Mull, Angus was surprised by a Maclean attack at his rendezvous at the south end of Kerrara, near Oban. Among the prisoners were MacDonald of Sleat, Macleod of Lewis, and 'McFee of Collowsay'.

Again the King tried to impose a settlement, but Angus MacDonald refused to hand over his eight hostages and was outlawed. Lachlan Maclean agreed terms with the king, but soon renewed the feud. In 1588 MacIan of Ardnamurchan, an ally of the MacDonalds of Islay, was to marry Lachlan Maclean's mother. During the wedding festivities Lachlan ordered all the MacDonalds present to be massacred. Only the bridegroom was spared. Then he raided the islands of Rum, Eigg, Canna and Muck – known today as the Small Isles. Apparently he made use of some Spanish mercenaries whose galleon was anchored at Tobermory on its way home from the debacle of the Spanish Armada. This expedition reportedly exterminated the population of the four islands. Angus MacDonald invaded Mull with a band of English mercenaries, but after some skirmishing an agreement was reached, and Angus exchanged his eight hostages for MacIan and some other prisoners.

The King had had enough. In 1589 the Macleans and MacDonalds were summoned to Edinburgh, arrested despite assurances of pardon for past offences, and promises were extracted. Angus MacDonald's son, James, was to remain in Edinburgh, where he became a favourite at court and was knighted. In the islands the peace held until only 1592, when a revolt of Scottish nobles diverted attention and tempted the feuding parties to resume hostilities. But parliament summoned them for treason in 1592, and sentenced them to forfeiture in 1594. Angus MacDonald, by now an old man, schemed with his kinsmen in Antrim and even with the English, but in the end gave in and agreed to behave himself, after his son Sir James MacDonald was sent from Edinburgh to reason with him.

But the exasperated King had leased the Rinns of Islay to Lachlan Maclean, which he was legally entitled to do since the MacDonald lands had been forfeited and so reverted to the Crown. In 1597 old Angus went to Edinburgh and made his peace with the King. He was to give up Kintyre and the Rinns of Islay, give security for payment of the arrears of Crown rents, and give up Dunivaig Castle to the King's nominee, while Sir James would remain at Court in Edinburgh for further security. Part of the settlement reads:

His Majestie sall have full libertie with the said Angus and his sonis consent, to dispone upoun the landis of Ilay noch sett to Makclane, and also upoun the haill ilis of Jura and Colanza and upoun the said fourtie merkland adjacent to Kilkarrane, as his Majestie sall think gud for planting of burrow townis with civile people, religioun, and traffique of merchandice thairupoun.

In other words, Civilisation was about to be imposed. But the failure of the MacDonalds to retain control of their ancestral holdings was to mean a serious upheaval on Colonsay and Oronsay.

SIR JAMES MACDONALD

Ironically, Sir James MacDonald was to be the main cause of this upheaval. Early in 1598 his father Angus had still not handed over his Kintyre estates, and Sir James decided to bring him to book. He cornered his father in his house at Askomel, at Kilkerran in Kintyre – now part of the Royal Burgh of Campbeltown, one of the 'burrow townis' envisaged by James VI. It was founded in 1609 and subsequently settled by reliable Protestant merchants and farmers from Ayrshire.

Sir James was determined to bring his father in, and old Angus walked unwittingly into a trap. Sir James was staying at the farm of Smerby, two miles north of Kilkerran, with his old friend John McKay, when his father arrived at Askomel from Islay. Hearing that his son was nearby, Angus walked over to Smerby to visit, spending over two hours in his son's company. No doubt suitably lubricated against the winter cold, it was after midnight when Angus left Smerby. By the time he got home to his house at Askomel, his wife was fast asleep in bed.

They and their household were rudely awakened 'about the dawning of the day' by a commotion outside. According to a contemporary witness, there were 300 men around the house, armed 'with hagbuittis, pistolletis, axes, bowes,

targeis, two handit swordis and uther invasive wapines'. The
door of Askomel House was securely locked and bolted, but
Sir James pounded on the door, demanding his father's surrender. Angus politely declined, whereupon his son and his
followers set fire to four different parts of the house.

Sir James's mother Finwall Maclean (Lachlan's sister)
and the rest of the household escaped unharmed, but the old
man refused to yield. But eventually he was forced to make
a run for it, or he would have been burned alive. As it was,
he was burned 'on three or four parts of his body and on
his shoulder', and his shirt was badly singed front and back.
Sir James had 'laid trees afore the house door purposely' to
cause Angus to 'fall on his outcoming'. Angus rushed out of
the house, tripped on the 'trees', and was duly captured. He
was put into iron chains, and imprisoned first at Smerby, then
in Saddell Castle for two nights, and finally safely delivered
to the royal castle at Dumbarton.

Sir James's accomplices in this escapade included his
younger brother Angus, the lairds of Largy and Loup, many
of 'Clanallaster' and what old Angus described as 'the haill
tennentis of Kintyre'. One complication was that Angus was
sheltering the two sons of the tutor of Loup. The Laird of
Loup had killed their father and was determined to murder
the sons as well. We do not know the reason for this feud,
but after a night of feasting and drinking at Smerby a punitive expedition to Askomel must have seemed a fitting end
to an entertaining evening. Unfortunately for Sir James, the
authorities did not share his enthusiasm. Public opinion was
outraged, old Angus was pardoned, and released on promises
of good behaviour, having suffered enough. Five years later
he turned the tables on his son; he captured him in Islay and
handed him over to Campbell of Auchinbreck, who took him
to the Earl of Argyll, who delivered him to the Privy Council
in Perth where, for his excess of zeal he was charged with
wilful fire-raising and treason.

After the outrage at Askomel, Sir James had fled to
Islay. Meanwhile Lachlan Maclean had decided to take

advantage of the MacDonalds' infighting to extend his hold
of Islay. In August 1598 the two sides fought each other at
the Battle of Traigh Gruineart, in which the Macleans were
routed and Lachlan Maclean was killed. Sir James himself
was wounded.

These are the facts as far as they are known in the
historical record. To be sure, these events contain more
turns and twists of fate than ever entered the mind of the
most imaginative soap-opera script writer. But according to
traditions preserved in Islay, the truth of what really happened at Traigh Gruineart was even stranger and weirder,
and it involved a MacDuffie.

BATTLE OF TRAIGH GRUINEART

The story is preserved in the family of Arra Fletcher of
Islay, handed down by word of mouth over the generations.
As the two sides were preparing for battle, a dark skinned
hunch-backed dwarf of a black, hairy appearance came to
Lachlean Maclean, and offered his services as an archer.
His father was a Shaw from Jura and his mother was a fairy
woman. He was called Dubh Sith; to the people of Islay, his
name meant 'black fairy'. He had to twist his ugly head to
look up at Lachlan, who stood over seven feet tall. Maclean
treated him with contempt, and declined his offer of help.
The Macleans outnumbered the MacDonalds and he was
confident of victory.

So, the dwarf sought out Sir James MacDonald, and
offered his services to him. This time, he was gratefully
received. The Dubh Sith said that if the MacDonalds looked
after the rest, he would take care of Lachlan Maclean. He
climbed up into a rowan tree beside a well, and waited.

The battle was fought on a hot, August day, and during
a lull in the hostilities Lachlan Maclean made his way to
the well for a cooling drink. As he removed his helmet and
knelt to drink, the Dubh Sith took his chance, and shot a
bolt from his crossbow straight into the back of Maclean's

neck at such an angle that the tip came out at his eye. With their leader dead, the Macleans lost heart, and when Sir James MacDonald was wounded, the MacDonald forces took the upper hand, and routed their opposition. The Macleans sought sanctuary at the church at Kilnave, but in their thirst for vengeance the MacDonalds set fire to the thatched roof. All the Macleans inside were killed, except for one man, a MacMhuirich (Currie), who ran into Loch Gruinart, and saved himself by submerging himself in the water and breathing through a reed. The MacDonalds thought he had drowned and left; later the exhausted man found his way ashore and was given shelter. His descendants still live in Islay, in Bowmore.

What are we to make of this tale? When clan historians put the story together, they needed some reason for Lachlan's defeat, and this they found in the idea that he had failed to heed the advice of a wise woman, who had told him not to land on Islay on a Thursday, and to stay away from Loch Gruinart and from the well known as Tobar Niall Neonaich (the well of strange Neil). Lachlan ignored these warnings; his arrival on a Wednesday was delayed for one day by a storm, he fought on the shore of Loch Gruinart, and he took a fatal drink at the prescribed well.

The magical motif is maintained by introducing the Dubh Sith, who was most probably not the son of a fairy woman but a MacDuffie with a physical deformity. Supernatural intervention, especially by the Devil, was often introduced in Highland folklore to explain mental or physical deformity. We have already seen in our consideration of the origin of the name MacDuffie that 'Shaw' is just another version of the 'Sithe' element in the name.

The Edinburgh authorities took a dim view of these events. The Scottish King was now the ruler of the United Kingdom, and is known to English historians as James I. As a major European monarch, it was not good for his image for stories of queer happenings and primitive warfare to be spread around the capitals of Europe.

At his trial in 1609, Sir James MacDonald was condemned to be executed as a traitor, and all his possessions were forfeited to the Crown. But the sentence of death was never carried out. Perhaps it was true that Sir James had had a personal commission from the King to bring his father in, and that in return for keeping silence on this point his life was spared.

In 1614 old Angus MacDonald died, possibly at Rothesay, and was buried, it is said, at Saddell. His younger son, Angus, was tried and condemned for high treason and executed at Edinburgh on 8 July 1615, for his part in an abortive uprising to restore the Lordship of the Isles. Sir James escaped from Edinburgh Castle in 1615 and briefly captured some of his lands in Islay, but then was forced to flee to Spain. In 1620 he was pardoned by the King, but forbidden to return to Scotland. He made his home in London with a state pension of 1,000 gold marks a year, and died there in 1626.

LOCH AN SGOLTAIRE

The tangible remains of Sir James MacDonald's campaigns can be seen on the small island on Loch an Sgoltaire. It is easily reached by a track leading up the hill from the entrance to Colonsay House. From the shore of the loch all that can be seen is the nineteenth century summer-house, but around it lie the walls of a defensive fort, exactly paralleled by one on a similar island on Loch Gorm, in Islay. It is thought that they were built by Sir James either after the events of 1598, when he anticipated a punitive government expedition, or more probably, in 1615 during his brief rebellion after his escape from Edinburgh Castle.

We must now examine more closely the reasons for Sir James MacDonald's rather desperate and predictably hopeless rebellion, because among its consequences were the ending of MacDuffie rule on Colonsay, the transfer of the MacDonald homeland of Islay to the Campbells, and a hundred years of social dislocation on Colonsay and Oronsay.

7 THE SEVENTEENTH CENTURY

A charter issued by James VI and I 'at Quhytehall' on 30 March 1610 granted the lands and island of Colonsay to Archibald Campbell, the 7th Earl of Argyll. The lands listed in this charter, with their modern equivalents, were as follows:

Ballenehard	(Balnahard)
Killoderans	(Kiloran)
de duabus Gilcattingis	(Upper and Lower Kilchattan)
Mauchrenecleif	(Machrins)
Balleveray	(Balavetchy)
Kilbreid	(Kilbride)
Maucherybeg	(Machrins)
Arskyinis	(Ardskenish)
2 Ballerymyn	(Balerumindubh and Baleruminmore)
Skallissage	(Scalasaig)

All these lands were granted to Argyll, along with the island's 'castles, manors, mills, fishings, lakes, ecclesiastical advowsons, benefices and chaplaincies'. An 'advowson' is the right of nominating a member of the clergy to a vacant benefice or living.

1615 REBELLION

Fortunately for the reader, there is not space in this volume to explore in detail all the intrigues and machinations which preceded the rebellion staged by Sir James MacDonald in 1615. However, the bibliography at the end of this book indicates some pathways for those with a special interest.

After a period of tortuous plots and counter-plots, Angus MacDonald, Sir James's younger brother, found himself besieged at Dunivaig Castle in Islay by a government force under the command of Sir John Campbell of Calder. They had brought ordnance from Edinburgh Castle, against which even the thick walls of Dunivaig proved useless. After only three days' bombardment Angus surrendered. He was subsequently tried for treason in Edinburgh and executed, with three others, on 8 July 1615.

Loder (1935) sums up nicely what had happened:

On the facts produced at the trial of Angus and those who were brought to Edinburgh with him, there is no doubt that the MacDonalds were victims of intrigue, in which the Bishop and the Lord Chancellor on the one hand, and the Campbells on the other, exploited the islanders' ignorance of the ways of the great world.

COLKITTO

But that was far from the end of the affair. One of the MacDonald supporters besieged at Dunivaig had been Coll Ciotach, 'Left-handed Coll', a proud and talented warrior to whom surrender did not come easily. Another meaning of Ciotach is 'crafty', and Coll certainly showed plenty of cunning in his career; as is often the case, his nickname was very appropriate. Colkitto, as he became known to the authorities, slipped away in a small boat during the night, along with some twenty followers. Six were captured when their leaky boat was forced to put ashore on the Oa peninsula, but Colkitto and the rest escaped, to fight another day.

Coll Ciotach and the ill-fated Angus were related; their grandfathers were brothers, descended from Iain Mor Tanister, younger brother of Donald, the second Lord of the

Isles. Coll was born in 1570, in Colonsay, at Kiloran.

When Sir James MacDonald escaped from Edinburgh Castle in May 1615, he made straight for his Islay homeland. Coll, meanwhile, was roaming the Hebrides, raiding and looting over a wide area. He and Sir James joined forces on the island of Eigg in the second week of June. Their combined forces totalled some 300 men. Heading for Islay, they arrived at Colonsay on 18 June, where a base was established, on the island in Loch an Sgoltaire. But a government spy was channelling intelligence to the Secretary of State, Lord Binning. On 20 June MacNeill of Taynish wrote: 'Sir James was four nightis in ane little yllan, callit Collinsaye, and slew ane numir of merttis (cattle). He has maid ane strength in it upon ane fresch watter loch in ane eyllane'. This, surely, refers to the fortified island in Loch an Sgoltaire.

By 29 July Lord Binning heard from Archibald Campbell, son of the prior of Ardchattan: ' I am certanelie informit be my spie that McFie of Collinsay, Donald gigache in Jouray, hes gone with the rebels and ar earnest transporting thair gudis to Ilay'. On the same day, he heard again from MacNeill:

Two speciall men that held of Argyle befoir ar newlie rebellit with thame, McDuphe of Collinson and his haill name, and Donnald Gigaich Makean who held Jura of Argyle, those two chiftanes ar gaine with the rebels thriescore and foure and remaines in Kintyre in pairtis neirest Argyll as zit making thair boast and wowing to be at the Tarbert quhilk is nyne myls within Argyle's boundis this night or the morne.

So, events were moving fast, and urgent and decisive action was called for if this rebellion was to be nipped in the bud. Meanwhile, the rebels decided to occupy Kintyre, hoping to hold the isthmus at Tarbert. It took a while for the government to get its act together, but in the end it was able to launch two attacks on the rebels. The Earl of Argyll moved south by land from his base at Duntroon, near Crinan, while Campbell of Calder launched a sea-borne assault on the main rebel camp, near Tayinloan in Kintyre.

What followed was more a series of skirmishes than a battle, but the scattered rebel forces were easily overcome, and their leaders fled. Coll made for the stronghold in Loch Gorm, in Islay, while Sir James, finding it impossible to land in Islay, went to Ireland. Coll then negotiated at the expense of his friends, eventually handing over nineteen men, including Malcolm MacDuffie of Colonsay, to Argyll.

Eventually everything was sorted out with no more bloodshed. Malcolm MacDuffie of Colonsay (now known to the government as Malcolm MacFie) was pardoned in 1618, and went back home. Colkitto submitted in 1619, was pardoned, and also went back to his home island of Colonsay. As we have mentioned previously, Sir James was allowed to return from Spain in 1621, though condemned to internal exile in London. The Earl of Argyll, who converted to Catholicism, also found himself in exile in Spain, where he and Sir James MacDonald are reported to have met. He too was eventually allowed to return to England, where he died in 1638.

MALCOLM MACFIE

There now followed a period when Coll Ciotach and Malcolm MacFie contested for supremacy on Colonsay. Clearly Malcolm had the support of the local population, while Coll had the military strength and prowess which he had used to such good effect during the 1615 rebellion. According to Loder (1935) there are at least seven places on the islands known as *Leab' Fhalaich Mhic a' Phi* – MacFie's Hiding Place:

– under the gable at the east end of the north wall of the priory church at Oronsay

– a small cave on the north-west side of Dùn Ghallain, on the Machrins golf course
– a recess above a narrow gully leading to the big corrie below the hill called *a' Chrannaig* (the pulpit), at Machrins
– another recess on the north slope of Carn Spiris, Ardskenish
– a sheltered hollow situated north-west of the houses at Lower Kilchattan
– behind another house at Kilchattan
– at Kiloran Bay

It sounds very much as if Malcolm was almost continually in hiding! But eventually Coll's men caught up with him, when they spotted Malcolm crossing to Oronsay. Malcolm could have had a head start of over a mile, if he was spotted crossing the Strand. This time there was nowhere to hide. Malcolm ran to the southern end of Oronsay, and swam across the narrow channel to Eilean nan Ròn, where he hid himself on the rocky shore under some seaweed.

Coll's men commandeered a boat and searched around the offshore rocks and skerries, but were unable to find him. But when they were on the point of calling off their search, assuming that Malcolm must have drowned, one of their party named Thomas Macillivoirichy noticed a sea-bird swooping over a patch of seaweed, shrieking in an agitated way, its attention attracted by something hidden in the rocks. In this way MacFie's last hiding place was discovered, and the fugitive was captured.

Local tradition has even preserved the conversation between MacFie and his captors:

Fàbhar, a Thàmhais
Fàbhar no fàbhar, is beag fàbhair a gheibhthteadh o t'fheusaig ruaidh mu'n àm so'n dé.

(Mercy, Thomas)
(None of your mercy; it's little mercy we would have got from your red whiskers this time yesterday!)

Unfortunately we don't know enough about Malcolm's previous escapades to know if Thomas Macillivoirichy's banter was justified. But presumably there was no love lost between the two camps, especially as Coll had handed Malcolm over to the authorities in 1615, and although Malcolm's life was spared, many MacDuffies must have been killed at that time.

Malcolm was taken to Pàirc na h-Eaglais at Baleruminmore, where he was placed against the tall cross-marked standing stone, and shot, along with four other men. He was the last recognised chief of the MacDuffies of Colonsay.

The judicial response was swift. On 27 June 1623 'Coill McGillispik McDonald in Collonsay, Archibald McDonald his sone, and four others, servitouris to the said Coill' stood trial, accused of participating 'airt and pairt of the fellone and crewall Slauchter of (the late) Malcolme Mcphie of Collonsay, Donald Oig Mcphie, Dougall Mcphie, Johnne Mcquhirrie, and Ewir Bayne, alias Quhyte; committit in Februar last'. The 'Perswaris' (Pursuers) are given: 'Marie McDonald, the relict' was Malcolm's widow. His daughters were 'Katerene, Anne and Fynwall'. Also mentioned is 'Murdoche Mcphie in Ilay', the brother of Donald Oig, and 'Dougall Mcphie, as nerrest of kyn to (the late) Johnne and Ewir'. This was a civil action for compensation, not a criminal prosecution for murder, and the verdict of the court reflects this: 'the Justice Ordanis that the saidis Coill, etc. sall be denuncet our souerane lordis rebellis, and all thair moveabill guidis to be escheit'.

Apart from the 'Perswaris' listed in Colkitto's indictment, nothing is known about Malcolm's family or immediated heirs, although a Donald McPhie had a lease of Colonsay and Oronsay in 1651. But to the many who claim descent from the MacDuffies of Colonsay, the stone at Baleruminmore is a place of pilgrimage, and throughout the year there is a steady trickle of visitors who come to pay their respects to their last chief.

Malcolm's burial place cannot be identified: no gravestone has been found to commemorate the last MacDuffie chief. He

127

could be buried in the old burial ground at Baleruminmore, or he could perhaps have been taken to Oronsay, to be laid to rest with his MacDuffie ancestors.

MacFies come from all over the world. One of the leading members of the clan is Ulf Macfie Hagman, a Swede of Scottish descent, who visited Colonsay in 1970, when the stone was lying broken and fallen. He determined to undertake the repair and restoration of this important piece of his clan history. Having already commented in chapter 5 on the unfortunate way in which the re-erection of the stone was done, it is unnecessary to belabour the point here. Indeed, although aesthetically displeasing, the idea of a plot of land commemorating the events of 1623 is appealing, and rather touching. Various obstacles were overcome, and the Carragh Mhic a'Phi was dedicated at a ceremony on 9 May 1977, in the presence of MacFies from all over the world. A glance at the Isle of Colonsay Hotel register for any year will show addresses in the USA, Canada, Australia, and New Zealand for many descendants of MacFies who emigrated to these countries in the eighteenth and nineteenth centuries.

There are Clan MacFie Societies in Scotland, Sweden, Canada, USA, Australia, and New Zealand, and they have created an international secretariat which organises events at regular intervals. The proprietor of the Isle of Colonsay Hotel in Scalasaig can supply current names and addresses of the secretaries of these bodies. In this context, it is appropriate to recognise the tremendous contribution of the late Dr Earle Douglas MacPhee of Vancouver, the driving force behind the resurrection of Clan MacFie societies and the author of various volumes which together make up *The Mythology, Traditions and History of the MacDhubhsith-MacDuffie Clan* (1975).

THE FRANCISCAN MISSION

In the years following the Protestant Reformation in Scotland, which took place in 1560, Colonsay and Oronsay were, as we have seen, on the very margins of effective control by central government. A series of remarkable documents survives in the Vatican Archives in Rome, covering the period 1619–46, and detailing the activities of Irish Franciscan missionaries in the Western Isles.

Most of the relevant documents have been reprinted by Giblin (1964) and translated from Latin. The instructions given by the Papal nuncio at Brussels to the missionaries about to leave for Scotland in 1623 summarise the situation:

> . . . there are many islands along the coasts of Scotland whose inhabitants have not seen catholics for a long time; they have no priest of their own, and there are no English or Scottish priests who can be of assistance to them, because such priests have no knowledge of Gaelic.

The missionaries were given some pointers as to which island lairds would be sympathetic to their cause:

> Col Makdonel [Coll MacDonald – Colkitto], the laird of Colonsay is a catholic, and he can provide the missionaries with information and give them directions as to how to visit the other islands.

Every year from 1623–31 the Franciscans made journeys throughout the Hebrides. In 1624 Patrick Hegarty and his companions travelled to Sanda, Kintyre, Arran, Gigha, Islay, Jura and Colonsay. In the course of the journey they brought 600 persons back to the faith. In Colonsay alone they re-converted 133 and baptised ten.

In 1625 Cornelius Ward, Paul O'Neil and Patrick Hegarty sailed from the island of Cara at the south end of Gigha to Oronsay. The voyage took twelve hours. They arrived at dark, sheltered overnight in a hut, and next day explored 'the ruins of a monastery' – only sixty-five years after the Reformation the priory at Oronsay was already a derelict ruin. They found that the Laird of Oronsay, a MacDonald, was a catholic, and in a short visit they re-converted forty souls and administered sacraments – presumably at the high altar in the priory church. Proceeding to Colonsay, they converted nineteen people, but had to leave because no food was to be had. The laird was not at home, and perhaps most of the local people were reluctant to get involved without his approval. The missionaries spent their last night on Colonsay on the beach in the open air, eating shellfish collected from the shore.

Next year they were back, and met 'Collatius Kiotach Macdonell' (Coll Ciotach MacDonald), his wife and daughter. They converted fifty in Oronsay, thirty-four in Colonsay, and baptised ten. They stayed for only three days because they heard that a Protestant bishop was on their track.

An undated document from this period, probably compiled in 1624, lists the names of catholics in Kintyre, Arran, Bute, Islay, Jura and Colonsay. It gives the names of 254 Colonsay people, 120 men and 134 women. This must have been very nearly the entire adult population of the island. Analysis of the names on this list reveals some surprises. There are only 4 MacDuffies (Mary, Neil, Daniel and Cecilia 'Dubhuy'), whereas there are already 16 MacNeills, 14 MacIains and 11 MacDonalds. The commonest surname is 'Muireadh' (Murray), with 21 entries, closely followed by MacKay with 20. Perhaps the most unexpected feature of the list is the tremendous variety of surnames (more than 85), although many of these derive from the person's father, and are not to be regarded as surnames in the modern sense. Among the less common names are Stockuir, Saoir (now Macintyre), Goban (Smith), MacEachern, MacCrimmon, Macmillan and MacSporran.

With forenames there is more consistency. Amongst the women the commonest names were Mora (23), Catarina (21), Mary (19), Nola (16), Christina (10), Margaret (9) and Aphrica (7). 'Aphrica', still found today as Efric amongst Gaels, is the Gaelic version of Euphemia. Other female names occuring less commonly are Anna, Elizabeth, Dorothea, Cecilia and Petronella.

The most popular male forename on Colonsay was Daniel (27), followed by Iain (16), Gillatius (11), Neill (9), Columba or Malcolm (9) and Aeneas (Angus) (8). Among the other names are Donatus, Christopher, Alexander, Thomas and Edmund.

The archive also contains a copy, in Latin, of a testimonial letter from Coll Ciotach concerning Ward and Hegarty, referring to his rescue of Ward from pursuing Protestants in 1629. It says that 'ministers and heretics' tracked him down, and that he had nowhere to go for protection, but Coll came to his rescue, at the risk of his life and the loss of goods, being severly wounded in the process.

These documents all survived because of a dispute over an expenses claim. The Papal authorities, and in particular the officials disbursing payments, took a sceptical view of Ward's claims, and there was a strong suggestion that he had not in fact made all the journeys claimed for, nor converted the numbers stated. The missionaries were supposed to get an annual financial allowance from the Congregation of Propaganda in Rome. The officials of this body insisted that in order to receive an allowance it was necessary that the missionaries report regularly on what work was being done. They complained that regular reports were not being sent, and withheld funds. On the other hand, the missionaries said that they were sending in regular reports, along with pleas for funds. Perhaps some of the reports were lost, or intercepted. However, to anybody who has ever tried to extract money from a bureaucracy, it all sounds only too familiar!

ALASDAIR MACCOLLA

Colkitto's son Alasdair was born, very likely in Colonsay, in the early years of the seventeenth century. It is said that swords rattled in their scabbards when he was born. He was fourteenth in a direct line of descent from Somerled. In the 1640s he made a great reputation for himself as a general in the army of James Graham, the Marquis of Montrose, who was trying to win Scotland for Charles I and the Royalist cause. He won a knighthood for his services to the king, and became known in the Lowlands as Sir Alexander MacDonald. As a fighting warrior-leader he was unsurpassed, though as a strategist he has been criticised as being too impetuous and insufficiently prepared for the aftermath of battle.

As Alasdair's career has been comprehensively covered in Dr David Stephenson's recent study, *Alasdair MacColla and the Highland Problem in the 17th Century* (1980), it is not necessary to detail the events of 1645–6. Montrose defeated six armies in the Covenanting Wars, and Alasdair MacColla was involved in all his campaigns. The winter campaign to sack Inveraray, the march over the hills in winter from the Great Glen to Inverlochy, and the battle of Auldearn are still admired by military historians. But Montrose was eventually defeated at Philiphaugh and Carbisdale, and Alasdair retreated to his Argyll homeland, pursued by General Leslie.

The final defeat of the campaign was at Rhunahaorine in Kintyre, near Tayinloan. Why Alasdair did not make a stand at the easily defended isthmus of Tarbert has always been a bit of a mystery. Marion Campbell of Kilberry makes the interesting suggestion that because he had broken his *geas* or taboo given to him by his nurse in Colonsay, he knew that resistance was futile and accepted his inevitable fate. We have already seen how Lachlan Maclean ignored his *geas* in Islay in 1598, and paid with his life. Alasdair's taboo was that he was never to raise his standard at a place named *Gocam-go*. But in 1647, encamped near Loch Awe, he found himself at precisely this place. It is said that 'his heart quailed and he became for a moment as a child'. According to traditions preserved in Kintyre, when General Leslie's armies attacked Alasdair's troops near Tayinloan, Alasdair was drinking beer in Largie Castle with MacDonald of Largie, to whom he was of course related. Seeing his troops overwhelmed by the Covenanting army, he abandoned them to their fate, and took ship for Islay and Ireland, where he was killed in battle later in 1647.

In fact, about three hundred of his troops, MacDougalls

from Lorn and local MacDonalds for Kintyre, managed to retreat in good order from the battlefield of Rhunahaorine, and sought refuge in the stronghold of Dunaverty, at the south end of the Kintyre Peninsula. Here they were besieged, and eventually agreed to an unconditional surrender. At the insistence of the army chaplain, all were put to the sword.

General Leslie's army then sailed over to Islay, where they besieged Dunivaig Castle, which was being held by Alasdair's father, Colkitto, now an old man of 77. As at Dunaverty, the garrison ran short of water in what must have been a dry, hot summer, and were forced to surrender. But this time there was no chaplain to insist on instant death for the heretics. The terms agreed were a promise of quarter for the garrison, freedom for the officers, and the transfer of the rank and file to France for enlistment in one of the Scottish mercenary regiments. While the talks were still going on, old Coll himself was captured by trickery by Campbell of Dunstaffnage.

He was taken to Dunstaffnage Castle, and sent for trial before George Campbell of Airds, the Sheriff Depute. He was condemned to death and executed at a place near Saulmore farmhouse (between Dunbeg and Connel) still known as *Tom a'Chrochaidh*, 'the mound of the hanging'. He is said to have been hanged from the mast of his own galley fixed across a cleft in the rock. Coll's other sons, Archibald and Angus, both fell into Campbell hands, and were also executed.

RESTORATION

The Restoration of the Monarchy in 1660 under Charles II produced some changes in Colonsay. As Coll and his family had supported the Royalist cause, the MacDonalds were suddenly back in favour. The heir to the Colonsay estates was Sarah MacDonald, the only surviving child of Coll's eldest son Archibald, so the lands of Colonsay and Oronsay were restored to her. But in 1663 Colonsay and Oronsay were granted as part of the barony of Ardnamurchan to Archibald,

Lord Lorn, son of the Marquis of Argyll, who now became the 9th Earl of Argyll, after the execution of his father for treason (for transferring his allegiance to Cromwell).

The islands remained under Campbell control until 1685. In 1681 the 9th Earl of Argyll was condemned to death for treason for supporting efforts to impose Episcopacy in Scotland. He subsequently escaped to Holland, and in 1685, after the accession of James II, he supported Monmouth's rebellion. After an abortive landing in the west of Scotland the 9th Earl was captured and executed.

So, in 1686, James II granted Sarah MacDonald a charter for Oronsay and Garvard, because of 'the singular bravery and constant fidelity' of Colkitto, her grandfather, in the cause of the King's father. But the revolution of 1688 brought still more changes. The 10th Earl of Argyll supported William of Orange, with the result that all the Argyll estates were restored to him and he was made a duke. Then, in 1695, we hear that the lands of Colonsay and Oronsay were leased for nineteen years to Neil McNeill of Taynish, and then in 1701 they were sold by the 10th Earl to Malcolm McNeill, eldest son of Donald McNeill of Crear in Knapdale.

The McNeills were to hold Colonsay and Oronsay for the next 203 years.

8 ISLAND LAIRDS

Although the islands were sold to Malcolm McNeill in 1701, in 1703 Martin Martin does not mention an island laird, but says that the islands were the property of the Duke of Argyll; according to Pennant, Colonsay was sold to the McNeills by Argyll in 1712. However, the documentary evidence for the transfer of ownership in 1701 is clear enough, and Loder (1935) gives a translation of extracts from the original Latin charter, which is in the possession of Lord Strathcona, the present proprietor.

Dated 6 March 1701, this charter records that Archibald, the first Duke of Argyll, granted 'the lands and island of Colonsay' and 'all and whole the island of Oronsay' to Malcolm McNeill for the sum of 21,000 marks. The annual feuduties, which were payable to the duke and his successors, amounted to the sum of six hundred marks for the 27½ merklands of Colonsay and Oronsay. The McNeills also had to to hold themselves in readiness to accompany the duke and his successors 'in hawkings, huntings, and military expeditions'. The charter also entitles Malcolm McNeill to the hereditary office of Bailliary, authorising the Laird to administer justice on the islands and, of course, to enforce the collection of rents.

Malcolm McNeill built Kiloran House in 1722. Little is known about the circumstances, but there is a passing reference in the *Statistical Account* of 1795, which is also of interest as another piece of evidence for some kind of religious community at Kiloran in the Middle Ages: 'the remains of the abbey were, with Gothic barbarity, torn asunder not many years ago, and the stones put into another building'. The *New*

Statistical Account (1845) says that the new house was built 'on the site of the old Culdee establishment there'. The 1722 mansion still forms the core of today's Colonsay House.

Malcolm's son Donald took over the estate on his father's death in 1742. Whereas in the seventeenth century Colonsay had become embroiled in the rebellions and wars which disrupted the whole country, in the eighteenth century the McNeills kept very much to themselves, and did not become involved in either of the Jacobite rebellions of 1715 or 1745–6.

BONNIE PRINCE CHARLIE

However, there is one intriguing piece of local tradition, to the effect that the Young Pretender, Charles Edward Stuart, better known as 'Bonnie Prince Charlie', did visit Colonsay en route from France to Scotland in 1745. Charles sailed from France in the *Du Teillay* (sometimes called the *Doutelle*) on 5 July 1745, heading for the island of Barra in the Outer Hebrides. There was a naval skirmish between his escort vessel and a British man-of-war on 9 July, another vessel was sighted on 11 July but quickly outdistanced, and land was sighted on 22 July. This was Barra Head. On 23 July, after picking up a pilot from Barra, the *Du Teillay* anchored in sheltered waters between Barra and Eriskay, and in the evening of that day the Prince first set foot on British soil on a beach on Eriskay. There is no mention in the *Du Teillay*'s log of any previous landfalls.

This, then, is the official history of these events, and none of the spate of books published in 1988 to mark the 200th anniversary of the Prince's death contradicted it. But the people of Colonsay tell a different story.

The tale of Bonnie Prince Charlie's visit to Colonsay was first published by Symington Grieve (1923). He says: 'I was told this story by so many old people on the island that I think there is no doubt about it being true'. According to them, a ship anchored near Eilean Olmsa at the end of July

1745. At that time Port Olmsa, which is on the east coast of the island about three kilometres/two miles north of the present harbour at Scalasaig, was used as a landing place, being handy for Kiloran House. An officer came ashore, and visited Donald McNeill at Kiloran to ask for his support, for permission to hide treasure for a military expedition on Eilean Olmsa, and to accept responsibility for its safe custody. The officer told Donald that the Prince was on board the ship, and that he had been told that it would be quite safe to leave his treasure at any place where heather grew, as the people could be trusted.

But although the Laird received the officer politely and treated him hospitably, he declined to get involved and asked for this message to be conveyed to the Prince. When Bonnie Prince Charlie received this news, he and several of his officers immediately landed on Colonsay and visited Donald McNeill at Kiloran House. After a prolonged discussion, the Laird refused to change his mind. The Laird's brother, Archibald McNeill, tried to explain that Colonsay was far too small a place to store treasure in. He also told him that he and his clan were loyal in their allegiance to Clan Campbell and the British Crown and would have nothing to do with the expedition.

The Prince then asked if McNeill would at least supply him with two pilots, to assist in navigating around the unfamiliar coasts and islands. McNeill told him that while there were suitably qualified men on the island, he did not know if they would want to get involved. But word quickly spread, and several candidates presented themselves to the Prince and his officers for interview. After a lot of haggling over terms and conditions, two Macmillan brothers agreed to act as pilots, in exchange for a small keg of gold coins each. They insisted that these kegs be landed in Colonsay and handed over to their relatives before they would board ship. Eventually, this was done.

But so much time had passed that darkness had fallen, and it was decided to spend another night at anchor off

Eilean Olmsa before setting sail. In talking to the crew Hector Macmillan began to get some inkling of what he had got involved with, and under cover of darkness slipped overboard and swam ashore. He kept his keg of gold coins, and prospered.

The other brother, Iain Macmillan, remained on the *Du Teillay* and served with the French throughout the Prince's time in Scotland. He is said to have married a French woman and settled at Dunkirk, where he later died. He wrote letters to his relatives on Colonsay but never returned home.

What are we to make of this story? With no reference in the official records, it could be dismissed as an invention, but the tradition is so widespread amongst Colonsay people, and the detail in the story so convincing, that one feels that there must be a solid core of fact behind the legend.

Other explanations could be offered for the story. There might be a confusion, for example, with the McNeill of Barra, who was away from home when the *Du Teillay* arrived at Barra. His lack of enthusiasm for the venture was well known. Then there is the fact that a pilot was recruited in Castlebay, who found a safe anchorage for the party and landed them successfully on Eriskay.

Taking another tack, it might have been some other French vessel that called on the Laird of Colonsay, perhaps leading the local population to believe that the Prince was on board in the hope of securing their co-operation. Perhaps somebody was trying to pass himself off as the Prince, either in an attempt to solicit intelligence, or for reasons to do with the Prince's security. Certainly there were several French ships in the area *after* Culloden, when they were trying to rescue the Prince and convey him safely to France.

A piece of corroborative evidence for the island tradition came to light from perhaps a not entirely unexpected source – North America. For Hector Macmillan's son, Malcolm Hector Macmillan (1751–1847) married Grace McNeill and emigrated to Canada in 1806 with ten children. This couple's eldest son, James, married and had fifteen children. Despite this, his wife lived to the age of 82. Her great-great-grandson, Douglas C. Macmillan, born in 1912, is the author of a family history, detailing all the American branches of the Macmillan clan who are descended from the couple from Colonsay who sailed to Prince Edward Island on the ship *Spencer* in 1806 and settled in Wood Island. Douglas Macmillan mentions the tradition in his family about Bonnie Prince Charlie in Colonsay, and about Iain Macmillan settling in Dunkirk. Perhaps Malcolm Hector (Calum Eachan in Gaelic) was able to use some of his father's keg of gold coins to pay for his passage.

Another small piece of circumstantial evidence comes from Murdoch McNeill, who when over ninety years of age told Symington Grieve in 1881 that his two grandfathers were among the few Colonsay men who were recruited in 1746 by the Hanoverian army. The Laird had been asked to send as many men as possible, but found the islanders reluctant to participate. In the end only eight joined up. They took their time getting to Inverness, travelling up the Great Glen at a leisurely pace. They arrived at their destination on the day after the battle of Culloden, and after a short time were sent back home.

MCNEILL REFORMS

One of the first 'tourists' to visit Colonsay and Oronsay was Thomas Pennant, who visited the islands in 1772 and met 'Mr Mac-neile' at Kiloran. He gives some details of agricultural practice. At that time there were no enclosures and no woods. The main crops grown were 'bear' (barley) and potatoes. 'Bear' was used in distillation, probably mostly exported for that purpose to Islay. Oats were sown in the middle of April, giving a yield of 3½ times the seed; for barley the yield was 8 times the amount sown; 'meal' was imported for subsistence; 250 cattle were exported annually at £3 a head.

From 40 to 50 tons of kelp were made annually, collected in April and exported in May, earning £3–4 a ton. Rabbit skins were exported – 1,440 a year. In the 1760s Kiloran Sands had been stocked with rabbits. Pennant thought that the human population of the two islands was between 500 and 600. In 1764 it was thought that Colonsay had 760 inhabitants and Oronsay 30. He visited the ruins of the priory – the plates from his book are among our major sources of information for our understanding of its architecture.

An abstract of the information Pennant collected on Oronsay in 1772 makes interesting reading. There was just one farm on the island, producing 'bear' (barley), flax, and 'much potatoes'. There were 60 milk cows, and 80 head of cattle, which sold at £3 a head. Butter and cheese were exported. The rent was £40 a year. There were 14 employees, whose function and annual remuneration are given by Pennant:

Chief Labourer	£2.10.00 + 1 stone (14lbs) of meal/week
Principal Herdsman	grass for 2 cows and meal for his family
Cow-herd	£2.4.0d + shoes
Assistant Cow-herd	16/-
Calf-herd	10/-
1st Aoireannan (herd) *and* 2nd Aoireannan	grass for 2 cows and 6 sheep, the 10th sheaf, 'produce of the ground', potatoes
Housekeeper	£3.0.0d
Principal dairy maid	12 marks Scots each ½ year
5 women	5 marks each ½ year

There were peacocks at Oronsay farm in 1772 – re-introduced in recent years.

One of the major sources for our understanding of life

in the Scottish islands in the late eighteenth century is the 12-volume *Statistical Account* of 1792. This project was the conception of Sir John Sinclair, who had the idea of getting the ministers of every parish in Scotland to send in an account of their parishes, covering various topics: religious history, antiquities, population statistics, industry and agriculture. It is a fascinating source of social history, varying from trivial to immeasurably valuable. Much of the material has been reprinted in a reorganised facsimile edition – in the original edition the reports from the various parishes were published as they arrived on the editor's desk, with no attempt to collate neighbouring parishes in the same volume. The indexing is rather haphazard, but a close study of the material throws up all kinds of interesting detail available nowhere else.

The contribution of the Rev Mr Francis Stewart, minister of the parish of Jura and Colonsay, is a mixture of stark fact and personal grievance. His problems arose from the scattered nature of his territorial responsibilities. From his manse in Jura he had to make regular visits to Colonsay and Oronsay, as well as to the islands of Scarba, Lunga and 'Balnahuaigh'. Out of his stipend of 2,000 marks he had to pay 800 marks to an assistant resident in Colonsay, though there was 'no proper house built for his accommodation, and there is no church to shelter the people from the inclemency of the weather'. The personal hardships and financial arrangements obviously weighed heavily on this isolated man of God:

> It is a peculiar hardship to the minister of Jura to be tied down to pay such a large proportion out of his benefice to an assistant-preacher, while he must, at the same time, incur the expense and danger of crossing broad perilous ferries to marry and baptize in the other islands.

Francis Stewart gives some details of the natural history

and agricultural economy of Colonsay and Oronsay. The soil is described as light and more fertile than Jura, giving 'uncommonly rich' pasture on low-lying and coastal areas. There were 'great numbers of rabbits in the islands,' in 1795, 'but no hare, no partridge, and very few grouse'.

The *Statistical Account* is a 'snapshot' of agricultural life in an age of improvement and revolution: in Colonsay and Oronsay, there were 15 farms in 1795, of which 7 were 'in tillage' and 8 in pasture, showing that the system of converting arable land into pasture was well under way. The best land was used for grazing cattle. There were no sheep on the islands, though Mr Stewart observed 'nature seems to have destined the heath-covered hills for their use'. A small, hardy breed of horses is also mentioned.

Pasture was fertilised either by 'great quantities of seacoral' found on the shores, or by seaweed, which was spread over grassland in winter, producing a luxuriant crop of clover and finer grasses. The farms were communities with an average population of 40 men, women and children. There were 134 families on Colonsay and Oronsay in 1795, and a total population of 718, made up of 352 males and 366 females, giving an average family size of 5.35. The inhabitants were described as 'robust and healthy'!

AGRICULTURE

A glowing account of the benefits to Colonsay and Oronsay of a hundred years of McNeill control can be found in the pages of the *General View of the Agriculture of the Hebrides or Western Isles of Scotland, with Observations on the Means of their Improvement*. The author is James McDonald, who was travelling on behalf of the Board of Agriculture. The results of his researches were published in 1811.

James MacDonald visited Colonsay in 1808. He was impressed by what he found there:

Collonsay is rapidly improving, more in consequence

of its proprietors exertions than of any natural advantages. . .Too much cannot be said in honour of the proprietors perseverance and industry in the improvement of the soil, as well as the live stock of this interesting island . . . Collonsay is famed for good farming, excellent cattle, and admirable economical management.

The object of all this praise was John McNeill, who was the Laird of Colonsay from 1805 to 1846. His portrait, by Thomas Duncan, is in the Scottish National Portrait Gallery. He was, says MacDonald, 'an enlightened, judicious and beneficent Highland proprietor'. It was he who added the long wing to the east end of Colonsay House, between 1820 and 1845, and erected the summer-house on the fortified island in Loch an Sgoltaire.

A 'thrashing mill' in Colonsay threshed six bolls of oats in two hours with three horses. A boll of oats weighed 160lbs and was reckoned to be the produce of one acre. The proprietor had introduced a regular system of tillage, with one man driving two horses, and encouraged crop rotation. The old system of tillage was for one man to walk backwards, leading four horses in line abreast. MacDonald had encountered this 'barbarous spectacle' all over the islands, and was pleased to see the new system being practised on Colonsay. Among the crops grown were barley, turnips, potatoes, and oats.

According to MacDonald, the rotation system for the first four years of newly reclaimed land was as follows: in the first year, break up with oats; in the second year, manure with turnips, beans, peas or potatoes; in the third year, barley with grass seeds; and in the fourth year, hay and forage. The rotation was then repeated.

McNeill's black cattle were particularly admired. In 1809 his three-year-old bullocks sold for £10.14s each, and he was rearing 200 calves each year, wintering 1,000 head in all. They were well fed, on turnips, potatoes and barley, and were housed in winter and in bad weather. In 1809 the island produced 1,500 tons of turnips and potatoes, and in addition there were 20 acres of sown hay. The manure used to fertilise the fields was seaweed, shell sand, dung from the animals, and composts made up of these materials.

A small kelp industry produced between 120 and 160 tons a year, and the weaving of flax into linen was a common cottage industry.

The number of horses on the island had been reduced under the new regime, from 230 horses to 100 work-horses, 23 mares and young colts. In 1808 there were no sheep farms on Colonsay, though many people kept them for their private use, especially for the wool.

MacDonald credits John McNeill with starting road-building on Colonsay; by 1808 he had already completed several miles at his own expense. The old road from Scalasaig to Kiloran was built at this time, as was the first harbour quay, in what is now Scalasaig harbour.

It was also John McNeill who was responsible for much of the tree planting that was to make the area around Kiloran so attractive. His predecessors had done some planting, but soon after 1805 ash, larch, sycamore, birch and rowan trees were established in large numbers and did well.

WAGES

Details are given in the *Statistical Account* of the price of labour in the islands. A male farm worker was paid £2 for a half year, while a female farm worker would get £1 for six months. A day labourer was paid six pence (ie 2½p) a day, 'and his victuals': the same terms applied to tailors and shoemakers. A boat carpenter was paid one shilling a day and victuals. Writing at about the same time, Robert Heron confirms these rates, adding that six pence a day was also paid for 'works of husbandry', and that the rate for a 'man servant' was £4 a year and for a 'female servant', £2 a year.

The actual circulation of money was very rare amongst

what the minister calls 'the lower classes'. In the absence of trade and with few manufactured goods available for purchase, most people did not live in a money economy. It was hoped that the growth of a fishing industry would bring cash into the area as catches were sold, and that the presence of money would encourage individual enterprise and stimulate the island economy.

By 1808 James MacDonald could report some changes, and many improvements, in the living condition of the people and in the way they were paid, in money or by slips issued by the estate factor, for their labour. There were incentives for bringing unimproved land into cultivation.

EMIGRATION

The Rev Stewart records that 'a considerable proportion of the inhabitants crossed the Atlantic' in the summer of 1791, and that in the following year

> . . . a few emigrated from Colonsay to America. Those who remain, give out that they are waiting only good accounts from their relations, and a proper opportunity of being transported to the other hemisphere. Pity it is that such numbers should bid farewell to their native country, when there is so great a demand for useful citizens; and their situation might be rendered more comfortable at home. . .the inhabitants do not feel that strong desire of bettering their circumstances, that would stimulate them to exertion of industry at home; they foster the notion of getting at once into a state of ease and opulence, with their relations beyond the Atlantic.

NEW STATISTICAL ACCOUNT

In 1845 an updated *Statistical Account* was published, but unfortunately the entry on Colonsay is rather scanty and

145

uninformative. The Laird is credited with having made great improvements:

> . . . he has not only turned the land formerly in tillage to the best account, but he has also reclaimed a vast extent of moors, hills, and peat mosses from a state of absolute waste to that of productive soil. He has introduced the improved system of husbandry, in the utmost latitude of the expression, into Colonsay, and his crops are among the best in the West of Scotland. Of late years he has drained a great extent of meadow land, and every year more of the barren land has been brought into cultivation, and several thousand roods of stone dikes have been built.

The land area is given as 9,000 acres, a slight underestimate, of which one-third was meadow or arable in 1845. It was reckoned that the islands were wintering 1,000 head of black cattle and exporting 200 calves a year. The population in 1835 was 839.

SMUGGLING

According to Lord Teignmouth (1836), smuggling was suppressed around 1811, by which time agricultural improvements were well under way. He says that the Laird was 'lord paramount and magistrate of the Island', and had 'gone the round with the excise officer, and expressed his determination to banish any transgressor from the island'. Lord Teignmouth met 'Mr Macneil' in 1836, noting that his son had built a house on Oronsay. The mansion house on Oronsay was built in 1772, but was possibly extended later.

NEW LAIRDS

In June 1841 James Wilson, on a tour of inspection as Secretary to the Fishery Commissioners, met John McNeill, 'the venerable old Laird himself – "Sole King of rocky Colonsay", and his hospitable lady'. Wilson also met 'Captain McNeill, younger of Colonsay', whose brother was Malcolm McNeill of Lossit.

Alexander McNeill

In 1846, John McNeill of Colonsay died, and the estate passed to his eldest son, Alexander, whom Wilson had met in 1841. It is not known why he did not want to take over the management of the estate, but in 1847 he sold it to his brother Duncan, who was born at Oronsay in 1793, for £39,980. Then, in 1850, Alexander McNeill, his wife and two of his young daughters drowned when the *Orion* was wrecked at Portpatrick in Wigtownshire. There is an inscribed stone to their memory in Oronsay Priory. He had one other daughter, and three sons, of whom the eldest, John Carstairs, eventually became the Laird of Colonsay in 1877.

Duncan McNeill, Lord Colonsay

Duncan McNeill was one of the most successful of the Colonsay McNeills. He had a distinguished career in the law. He was Dean of the Edinburgh Faculty of Advocates, then Solicitor-General for Scotland and Lord Advocate in Sir Robert Peel's first two administrations, and was the member of Parliament for Argyll from 1843 to 1851. The *Dictionary of National Biography* says he 'enjoyed a lucrative legal practice, especially in House of Lords appeals.' In 1851 he was appointed an Ordinary Lord of Session. Then in 1852 he became Lord Justice-General and Lord President of the Court of Session. As a law lord, he took the title Lord Colonsay. When he was made a peer in 1867 he became Baron Colonsay and Oronsay, but as he died unmarried in 1874 at the age of 81, this title died with him. It is his monument which overlooks Scalasaig.

Two marble busts of Duncan McNeill, Lord Colonsay, were made by HM Sculptor for Scotland, Sir John Steell. This artist created the sculpture of the Duke of Wellington which stands in Edinburgh outside the Scottish Record Office

– 'The Iron Duke in bronze by Steell'! One of the busts used to be in the courthouse at Inveraray, where it was unveiled in 1874 by the Lord Chancellor, Lord Selborne, but it is now in private hands. The other is in the Scottish National Portrait Gallery, in Edinburgh. It is a .6m (2ft) high bust in white Italian marble, standing on a pedestal of polished Aberdeen granite. There is also a portrait in the same gallery, by Thomas Duncan.

It was Duncan McNeill, Lord Colonsay, who built the mill at Kiloran. The old mill, dating from before 1750, stood near the dam of the garden pond nearest Colonsay House. During the twenty-three years that he was Laird, economic conditions deteriorated steadily, though Colonsay was never as badly affected as other Hebridean islands. However, the island was now seriously overpopulated, and emigration to the Lowlands of Scotland and farther afield, to North America and Australasia, became common.

In 1870 Duncan McNeill sold the estate for £40,000 to his younger brother, John, who maintained it for only seven years, before selling it in 1877 to his nephew, John Carstairs McNeill, the son of Archibald who had drowned in the *Orion*.

Sir John McNeill
Sir John McNeill married three times: to Innes Robinson (1814), Elizabeth Wilson (1823) and to Lady Emma Campbell, sister of the Duke of Argyll (1870). He served the British East India Company for many years, and was the British minister to Persia. Returning home, he became the owner and lord of Colonsay, though was never, of course, entitled Lord Colonsay. Colonsay House still contains pictures and other objects brought back from Persia. He had only one child, a daughter, Ferooza, born in Persia in 1834. She died in 1871: a commemorative stone is in Oronsay Priory.

She was the wife of Commander Stewart, who kept Judge Campbell company on the steamer in 1873: Sir John McNeill was the Laird when Judge W. W. Campbell of the USA travelled to Colonsay in 1873 on the weekly steamer from Glasgow, arriving at midnight, in company with Commander Stewart, 'late of the Royal Navy', the son-in-law of the 'good old laird' of the island. They were transported to Kiloran in a private coach. Judge Campbell appreciated his 'genuine Scottish welcome'. He described his host as 'tall, erect, with white flowing locks; with a clear complexion, showing no marks of an Asiatic sun; with faculties unimpaired, though in age beyond fourscore years; with so many reminiscences of life in the East, and much quaint Scotch humor'.

A visiting naturalist and sportsman, Alfred Erskine Gathorne-Hardy, gives us an interesting verbal portrait of Sir John McNeill in a book published in 1914, regretting that Colonsay would no longer be able to enjoy 'his upright gait, his abrupt and alert manner, his kindly face, and to hear his brusque but ever genial welcome'. He details the use to which the added wings of 'Killoran House' were put. In one was 'a suite of bedrooms and servants' offices, and a comfortable smoking- and gun-room'. In the other, a billiard-room, library, dining room and drawing room. There were busts and portraits of various McNeills in the dining room, including a portrait of Sir John McNeill by HRH Princess Louise, Duchess of Argyll. A bust by Sir John Steell is in the Scottish National Portrait Gallery.

Sir John McNeill sold the estate in 1877 to his nephew for £80,072. He died in 1883, aged 88.

Major-General Sir John Carstairs McNeill

Deprived of his Colonsay inheritance in 1847, John Carstairs McNeill made a career in the army. He was involved in the Indian Mutiny, won his Victoria Cross in the Maori Wars in New Zealand, took part in the Red River expedition in Canada, was wounded in the Ashanti War of 1873–4, and won the battle of Tophrik during the Sudan campaign of 1885. He died, unmarried, in 1904, and was buried at Oronsay. Photographs of his funeral can be seen in the Isle of Colonsay Hotel.

After he retired from military life in 1890 he became an

equerry to Queen Victoria and ADC to the Duke of Cambridge. As a result of his acquaintance with the royal family, King Edward VII visited him at Colonsay on 30 August 1902, during the cruise in the royal yacht following his coronation. It was a great day in the history of Colonsay. Most of the island gathered to see the King and Queen land at Scalasaig. The King and Queen planted rhododendron bushes in the garden of Colonsay House, and the King is reported to have said that the figure on the little stone cross at St Oran's well resembled the chief engineer on the *Victoria and Albert*. After lunch the royal party re-embarked and resumed their cruise.

The *Oban Times* reported the day's events in detail:

> Flags were to be seen on every home and knoll in Scalasaig, while an arch of flags of various hues and patterns was stretched across the handsome pier . . . The people assembled amid a downpour of rain, early on Thursday, all arrayed in their best.

About seven o'clock the royal yacht, with attendant warships, entered the harbour. The evening was calm and wet. Early on Friday, word passed that the King would be ashore by 11 o'clock. It was a delightful day – not a cloud in the sky. Seven or eight islanders were presented to the King. The royal party, some in carriages, some on bicycles, went to Kiloran, 'amid the cheering and shouting of the people'. 'The people adjourned to the lawn in front of the hotel and drank right heartily the Health of the King and Queen and Royal Family'.

There are many legacies of the McNeill lairds. In Colonsay House their library survives more or less intact, with hundreds of eighteenth century books on a wide range of topics, including the relatively new science of agriculture, as might be expected. Regrettably, the estate papers do not appear to have survived. A map of the estate prepared in 1804 by Daniel Walker, a well known surveyor, is in the Scottish Record Office in Edinburgh. It identifies the different types of land, with a view to improving land wherever possible.

As would be expected from such a large family, many descendants of the McNeill lairds still exist. The father of the Duchess of Buccleugh was John McNeill, who was a nephew of the last McNeill laird, while General 'Jock' McNeill is probably the best known descendant in this country. The direct heir, Duncan McNeill, died in New Zealand in 1988. And lastly, there are undoubtedly people on Colonsay today who are descended from McNeill lairds, though we must circumspectly draw a veil over that particular side of the blanket! Many of the McNeills on Colonsay today descend, not from the McNeill lairds, who after all only came to the island in 1701, but from McNeills who were living there before Malcolm McNeill of Crear bought the estate.

DONALD SMITH

The present laird is Donald Euan Palmer Howard, the 4th Baron Strathcona and Mount Royal. Lord Strathcona inherited the title in 1959, on the death of his father. His great-grandfather was Donald Alexander Smith, born in 1818 in the small town of Forres on the Moray Firth, the second son of a local merchant. He left Scotland at the age of eighteen to work for the Hudson's Bay Company in Canada, and in twenty years rose from clerk to chief executive, at their headquarters in Montreal. He was a founding director of the Canadian Pacific Railway, High Commissioner for Canada in London, a member of the Canadian Parliament, Chancellor of MacGill University, and reputedly the richest man in Canada. He received honorary degrees from no fewer than fifteen universities in England, Scotland, Ireland, the United States and Canada. He had the honour of driving in the final spike of his railway, at Craigellachie in British Columbia on 7 November 1885. For many years a souvenir spike was proudly displayed in Colonsay House, but on the centenary of the ceremony the Strathconas presented it to the railway, for display in a museum in Canada. It is indeed the case that brooches worn

151

by the ladies of the family contain tiny pieces of iron from the Craigellachie spike incorporated into their design – along with the more usual diamonds, emeralds and rubies!

Donald Smith was rewarded for his enterprise with a peerage, bestowed by Queen Victoria in 1897. Wanting to acquire an estate in Scotland, he bought Glencoe, and it is impossible to conceive of anywhere more 'Scottish'. This remained the family seat until 1930. 'Strathcona' is a rather pretentious variant of 'Glencoe', while 'Mount Royal' derives of course from Montreal, in Canada. Colonsay was acquired as an afterthought, almost as a personal favour. When the last McNeill laird, who had paid far too much money for the estate, died in 1904, Lord Strathcona, who had previously lent him money, made a generous offer for the estate. Faced with clearing enormous debts, the McNeill heirs really had no choice but to dispose of Colonsay. Strathcona paid £44,000, writing off the £40,000 he had lent previously.

Donald Smith died, without a male heir, in 1914. By an arrangement known as a 'special remainder', granted in 1900, the title was transmitted through his daughter, Margaret Charlotte, whose husband, Robert Howard, was a medical doctor in Canada. Their son, Donald Sterling Palmer Howard, the father of the present Laird, became the 3rd Baron in 1926. In 1922 he had married Diana Evelyn Loder, the third daughter of the 1st Baron Wakehurst; her brother was John de Vere Loder, later Lord Wakehurst, Governor of New South Wales and Northern Ireland, whose 1935 book on Colonsay and Oronsay is the starting point for all subsequent research on any aspect of the islands. He also wrote *The Truth about Mesopotamia*, and was co-author of a thriller (with Francis Beeding). It was his family who brought to Colonsay the rhododendrons that adorn the grounds of Colonsay House.

The 3rd Baron Strathcona was a kindly man, whose major fault was his generosity. He was the laird during World War II, when Colonsay lay in a Prohibited Area and access was strictly controlled. The story is told that on arriving at Oban pier from Colonsay in darkness, he was challenged by a sentry and asked to identify himself: 'Lord Strathcona and Mount Royal', he replied, whereupon the sentry is reported to have said, 'Lord Strathcona, pass; Mount Royal, show me your papers!'

He served in the 1914–18 war, in which his brother Robert was killed, and held various offices of state thereafter. Before succeeding to his title he was a member of Parliament for North Cumberland, 1922–6. From 1925–7 he was Parliamentary Private Secretary to the First Lord of the Admiralty, and a member of the Indian Statutory Commission, 1927–30. In 1934 he became Parliamentary Under-Secretary of State for War and Vice-President of the Army Council.

The present Laird is a kindly, benevolent man, like his father, but more hard-headed. He has placed the running of the estate on a sound economic basis, since taking over the title in 1959, thanks largely to the development of self-catering accommodation on a large scale. In this enterprise he has been ably assisted by his wife Patricia, whom he married in 1978, having divorced from his first wife, Lady Jane Mary Waldegrave, the second daughter of Earl Waldegrave, the previous year. Parts of Colonsay House and adjoining service buildings have been converted to nine holiday flats, and in addition there are seventeen other properties around the island run by the estate as holiday houses.

These properties are fully booked for twenty-seven weeks in the year, meaning of course that most of them are empty during the winter months. The problem of housing is difficult, and causes more friction than anything else on the islands. Building council houses, or the council buying estate cottages for use as council houses, does not seem to be an answer as long as tenants can, after a time, buy their houses from the council and later re-sell them at a substantial profit to incomers for whom Colonsay is a desirable location for retirement or for a holiday home. If Colonsay Estate were ever sold or broken up, market forces would operate and it is unlikely that local people would ever be able to afford to buy houses on the island. Colonsay and Oronsay desperately need young couples with children, but at the moment providing housing is nearly impossible.

Despite the social and cultural gap between the Laird and the islanders, he and his wife do not assume airs and graces. He can often be seen in the harbour at Scalasaig, doing what he enjoys best – messing about in boats. He got plenty of practice at this during the war, in motor torpedo boats. After the war, in conjunction with a business career, he became heavily involved in politics in Edward Heath's administration. He was a government whip in the House of Lords, then Parliamentary Under-Secretary of State for Defence (RAF) in the Ministry of Defence in 1974. After the fall of the Heath government he served as joint Deputy Leader of the Opposition in the House of Lords from 1976–9, and became Minister of State, MoD, from 1979–81, when he lost his job in one of Mrs Thatcher's reshuffles. As a backbencher in the House of Lords, he frequently attends sittings and takes an active part in proceedings.

The son and heir is Donald Alexander Smith Howard (Alex), who has taken over the running of the estate (apart from the self-catering aspect), after seven years as a helicopter pilot in the Royal Navy; at the same time he is developing his expertise in financial matters through a career in the world of business and finance.

SOCIAL LIFE ON THE ISLANDS

In the years after the horrors of World War I, visitors to Colonsay and Oronsay indulged themselves in some rather daft ways. The Colonsay Yacht Club and Golf Club, both of which are still flourishing, afforded many opportunities for good-natured competition. Various clubs were formed, and crests and notepaper created. The Colonsay Swimming Club's motto was 'Only Death', meaning that only death would prevent the morning bathers from diving off the jetty at 8 o'clock. The Colonsay Lawn Tennis Association, (telegraphic address: 'LOVEALL') gave the address of its headquarters as 'Wimbledon Park, Uragig, Colonsay'. Its patron saint was Rachel, 'chosen because of her great contribution to the game – we were told she served the Lord for 40 years'. And so on. Regulars formed a society, whose 'logo' YLF can still be seen around the islands. This stood for 'You're Looking Fresh' and was based on the 'Y' on the products of Younger's Brewery. The 'Hon. Council of Colonsian Thiefs' was created in 1922: its crest incorporates a combination battle-axe/bottle opener. Its main function, according to one of its founder members, was to help 'while away the time in the long night journey round the Mull of Kintyre'.

It was all rather silly, but harmless, and very indicative of the class of tourist coming to Colonsay at that time. The Colonsay Hotel has a YLF crest over the bar, and many of the photographs around the hotel showing young men and woman participating in the various events and functions were taken by George Ward, a photographer of considerable technical skill. He had a camera which could take panoramic views – the lens moved as the picture was being taken.

9 SOCIAL HISTORY

RELIGION

Christianity has been a central pillar of island society for most of the last two thousand years, but in the period following the great social upheaval of the Protestant Reformation, the promotion of the Christian religion by its Protestant adherents was neglected in many of the more remote islands. In many communities, including Colonsay and Oronsay, it took about one hundred and fifty years for the new religion to take root.

Pennant thought that from 1560–1766, the sacrament had only been administered once. The Church faced considerable logistical difficulties both in providing a reasonable standard of service throughout such a large and fragmented parish and in maintaining discipline among both its members and its ministers.

The situation which the Irish Franciscans had turned to their advantage did not really change until the end of the seventeenth century. Meeting at Iona in 1656, the Synod of Argyll commented on the 'sad and deplorable conditione of the Ile of Collonsay'. There was no parish minister, and ministers from Mull and Islay would not carry out marriages or baptisms in the absence of properly constituted 'testificans' who could give supporting evidence, with the result that there were 'many fornicators in the country' and 'many children unbaptised'.

The Presbytery records for 1691 noted that Mr John McSwine (MacSween), an incumbent minister for Gigha, Jura and Colonsay, 'is guiltie of frequent scandalous drunkennes, and negligence in discharging ministeriall duties'. His life was made slightly easier by detaching the island of Gigha from the parish, but worse was to come. In 1697 he appeared before a Presbytery meeting at Kilarrow in Islay to answer charges that 'in Colonsa in presence of several gentlemen and others after drinking of aquavite to excess and the bottle ending sooner than he desyred, he chapped on it with his hand and said that the devil put the bottome out of it'. This might seem to many people a reasonable remark to make in the circumstances, but after evidence was heard, McSwine was found guilty of this charge (and others) and suspended from his pastoral duties.

In an attempt to regularise the situation, the Presbytery of Kintyre ordained in 1702 that 'the minister shall preach six months and a half in Jura, and five and half months at Colonsay, yearly'.

The problems of the Colonsay minister in the 1790s have already been alluded to. Things were made slightly easier after the new parish church was built in 1802. The architect was Michael Carmichael, and to pay for the church the sum of £444.11s.2d was raised from the heritors of the parish of Jura and Colonsay. A further £41.15s.2d was required for fittings and furnishings, and repairs totalling £30 were necessary in 1834. It was designed to seat 400 persons.

As it is today, this church is somewhat altered from its original design. On the south wall external stairs once gave access to lofts at each end of the building. These have been removed. Inside the church is a memorial to three islanders killed in the 1939–45 war, and there is also a chair made out of mahogany washed up at Port Lobh in 1948.

By 1833 there was a permanent assistant at Colonsay, and the minister's stipend in 1843 was £50 a year. Colonsay and Oronsay were joined with Jura until 1861, when they acquired separate parochial status. James Bannatyne MacKenzie was appointed minister, and served until 1872, when he was, in the language of the Church of Scotland, 'translated' to Kenmore in Perthshire.

From 1873 to 1881 the minister was Donald Maclean; after moving on to Harris, he was replaced by Dugald Carmichael. The son of Donald Carmichael, schoolmaster at Saddell, Kintyre; educated at Saddell School and Glasgow University, Dugald Carmichael was the minister of Colonsay and Oronsay until his death in 1915 – a lengthy and influential period of tenure.

In 1917 Kenneth Macleod came to the island and ministered there until 1925; author of the words of 'The Road to the Isles', he is probably best remembered for the three-volume *Songs of the Hebrides* (1908–21), produced in collaboration with Marjory Kennedy-Fraser.

Subsequent ministers have been Samuel Lipp (1954), Alasdair MacInnes (1957), Frederick Hurst (1965) and Ronald Crawford (1973). Mr Crawford left in 1988, due to ill health.

BAPTISTS

About 1812 the Baptist minister Dugald Sinclair visited Colonsay in a small sailing boat. He held meetings throughout the island, with good results. On leaving for Islay his boat was repeatedly driven back by stormy weather, leading him to believe that the Lord had need of him in Colonsay, or perhaps that Colonsay had need of the Lord!

In 1813 Sinclair returned, and made some converts, who were baptised by immersion in Loch Fada. One of them was John MacMillan, the son of the Laird's butler. He later went to college and was sent as a Baptist missionary to Inveraray. One can understand that they had more need of him there. Another convert was Neil MacEachern, but on his way to Mull in a small boat a great storm arose, and he and all on board perished.

Sinclair was the minister of the Baptist congregation at Lochgilphead, but made regular visits to Islay, Mull, Colonsay and the other islands of the Inner Hebrides. For many years he continued to make annual visits to Colonsay.

On one occasion the factor was sent to tell an assembled meeting that 'any person who attends this man's meetings or listens to his preaching will lose his lands'. But Sinclair pointed out to the factor that this kind of threat was against the law of the land, and the factor told the Laird that he would not carry out his instructions in this matter. Subsequently Sinclair invited himself to dinner with the Laird, and it is said they became good friends.

At least, the Laird's two daughters were converted. One was baptised in Edinburgh and the other in Loch Sgoltaire, by a Mr Grant of Tobermory. A minister was appointed in Colonsay, a local man, Malcolm Blue. He took the services for many years, assisted by Malcolm McNeill, the manager of Oronsay. McNeill took Bible readings and was responsible for leading the singing, though it is said he only knew three tunes! Another useful member was Duncan McDougall, who settled in Tiree after missionary training but was a frequent visitor to Colonsay.

The family of Lachlan McNeill all attained positions of importance in the Baptist church. John went to Canada, followed a few years later by the rest of the family. This was in 1852, when nine Colonsay Baptists emigrated to Canada. John was the father of John McNeill of Toronto, a famous Baptist preacher on both sides of the Atlantic. Lachlan's other sons, Donald (who was 2m/6ft 6in tall) and Alexander both became preachers.

Malcolm Blue died in 1858, while Malcolm McNeill died in 1873, in his eighty-fifth year. In 1879 the present chapel was built, to seat 100. In 1926 the membership was 25, but today only a handful of locals keep this branch of Christianity going: summer visitors are a more receptive audience.

KILCHATTAN BURIAL GROUND

There is just the one cemetery currently in use on Colonsay, at the burial ground surrounding the old medieval parish church at Kilchattan. Sadly, too many old folk die in hospital in Oban. This is a problem common to many Scottish islands, but Colonsay is too small to provide an alternative. At Kilchattan the history of the island is written on the gravestones. Here is the last resting place of John McNeill, miller, who died in 1892 at the age of 54; his wife Flora McPhee died in 1914 at the age of 65, thankfully spared from mourning the death of her two sons, both killed in 1917.

Murdoch McNeill, manager of the Colonsay Estate for forty years, died in 1904 at the age of 65. His stone is inscribed 'a trusted servant and friend – erected by Sir John C. McNeill, Proprietor'. Nearby is the grave of Malcolm McNeill, for 58 years gardener at Colonsay House, who died in 1910 aged 76. Another Murdoch McNeill (1873–1959) is commemorated by a stone erected by An Comunn Gaidhealach, the society trying to preserve Gaelic language and culture. He was the author of *Colonsay, its Plants, Climate, Geology, etc* (1910) and was a goldmine of information on folklore and local language and traditions. Roger McNeill, MD, DPH, JP, County Medical Officer for Argyll is buried here, and John McNeill (1803–75), for forty years a miller on Colonsay, along with his son, a marine engineer.

Donald Clark of the Scalasaig Hotel and his wife Catherine McPhee have an interesting stone. He died in 1934 at the age of 80, while his wife died the following year. Their four sons and two daughters are buried with them. One son was killed in 1918, another became a Master Mariner. Their daughter Mary died in 1986, aged 82.

Donald (Gilbert) McNeill died in 1918, aged 73, while his wife Margaret (Pegi Bhan) died in 1921, aged 71. With so many McNeills on the island each had his or her own nickname or by-name, and these are sometimes inscribed on their gravestones, for these are the names by which they were known. Gilbert and Pegi Bhan ('fair Peggy') had a son who died in France in 1915 and a daughter who died in Saskatoon, Canada, in 1938. Another daughter died in 1953, while Annabella died in 1962, aged 96.

Still another Donald, the 3rd Baron Strathcona and Mount Royal (1892–1959), father of the present Laird, has an imposing yet simple stone at Kilchattan.

One of the finest stones at Kilchattan is the memorial in the form of a Celtic cross to Professor Donald MacKinnon (1839–1914), the first holder of the chair of Celtic studies at the University of Edinburgh.

There are some military graves, dating from both World Wars – sailors whose bodies were washed up on the shores of Colonsay. Some are not identified. There are three of the crew of HMS *Viknor*, lost on 13 January 1915, and one from HMS *Blake*, lost on 21 August 1918. From World War II there are five from HMS *Transylvania* (10 August 1940), including a 'Barkeeper and Donkeyman'. Five further unidentified graves date from this tragedy, along with the graves of another two found on 26–28 September 1944, and a crewman from the SS *Empire Tiger* (27 February 1941). They lie alongside Walfrido Sagramati, 'morte per la Patria' on 6 August 1940, and a member of the Danish Merchant Navy, Birger Oest-Larsen, who was found on 6 January 1942.

Such was the toll of life in the North Atlantic that similar graves can be found on any Hebridean island.

Apart from the human cost in death and long separation, Colonsay was involved in a peripheral but important way in the global warfare of 1939–45. A small unit was set up at Machrins to communicate with North Atlantic convoys, and an immensely powerful beacon light was set up above Scalasaig to help transatlantic aircraft movements in their navigation.

ORONSAY BURIAL GROUND

There are still burials at the burial ground adjoining Oronsay Priory. However, the majority of the gravestones there are not inscribed, but are simple, small stones marking now forgotten graves. The McNeill Lairds have their own burial place, built on to the side of the priory. An inscription tells their story:

In this chapel are buried Malcolm McNeill who succeeded his father Donald McNeill of Crear in 1701; Barbara Campbell of Dunstaffnage and two of their sons; Alexander of Oronsay with his wife Mary McDougall of McDougall and Angus, Captain in the Army; also John McNeill son of Alexander, died 24th February 1845; his wife Hester McNeill of Dunmore, died 16th June 1843; and his brother Malcolm McNeill, died 10th August 1850.

Nearby is a memorial to 'Major General Sir John Carstairs McNeill, CCVO, KCB, KCMG, VC, JP and DL for Argyllshire, 27 years equerry to Queen Victoria'. He died on 25 May 1904, aged 73. His subsequent funeral on Oronsay was attended by many dignitaries and most islanders. Photographs taken of the funeral procession and ceremony can be seen in the Isle of Colonsay Hotel.

Also buried here is Margaret Ferooza McNeill, daughter of Sir John McNeill and the wife of Duncan Stewart, RN. She was born in Persia in 1834, while her father was stationed there, and died in Edinburgh in 1871. The stone was erected by her surviving children in 1891. Her husband, Duncan Stewart, featured in a celebrated court case in 1873, described below.

SCHOOLS

We know from the *Statistical Account* that there was a 'charity school' in Colonsay in 1795; the schoolmaster's salary was £15 a year. The minister saw the school as being 'of prodigious service towards enlightening the understanding, and improving the heart of a generation, that otherwise would be neglected'. The language of instruction of course was English, which was seen as 'of great service for life', although in their daily life everybody spoke Gaelic, and most of the older people understood no English at all.

In 1808, James MacDonald inspected the school and found that there were 78 scholars, 64 male and 14 female.

Another 24 children were taught privately, as they lived in parts of the island too remote from the parochial school.

Lord Teignmouth's *Sketches of the Coasts and Islands of Scotland* appeared in 1836, and contains some observations on Colonsay, including information on two schools. He says that instruction at the parochial school was in Gaelic, but that English was used at the SPCK school at Scalasaig, where there were 50 students. Fees were 1s 6d per quarter for reading, 2s for writing, and 2s 6d for arithmetic.

The present primary school at Kilchattan has just one teacher and normally fewer than ten children. A school bus tours the island in the morning, collecting children and delivering milk and eggs around the island. The two Oronsay children meet the bus on the Colonsay side of the Strand – just getting them that far is a major logistical problem. Depending on the tides, they are delivered to the road end either by tractor or boat, and they have to be met after school and transported home. Their father is thinking of buying a small hovercraft, which would be the perfect vehicle for coping with the full range of tidal conditions.

The schoolteacher has to teach children at different levels, but as at many other Scottish rural schools, the system works superbly well and the children come out of their island school with an amazingly well-rounded education. The children are well informed on their local history and traditions and produce a monthly news sheet for the island. Periodically there are trips to Oban, or even to Glasgow and Edinburgh. Asked to comment on the major differences between Colonsay and Glasgow, the children were unanimous – 'the smell in the city is horrible'. On one trip to Glasgow, while waiting to escort her flock across a busy junction in the city centre, the teacher suddenly realised that there were more people waiting there for the 'Green Man' than there were on the whole island of Colonsay!

After their primary schooling is completed, the children go to Oban, or to private schools further afield. This is one of the saddest aspects of living on Colonsay, and has a lifetime effect on children and parents alike. Colonsay is a very close-knit community, where the children are known to everybody. Their sudden removal to the mainland at the age of 11 or 12 is a terrible wrench for all concerned.

CRIME

In the early days the word of the Laird was law, and there were few complications. Lord Teignmouth (1836) reported that 'Mr Macneil is lord paramount and magistrate of the Island. He has effectually suppressed smuggling during twenty-five years, having at the commencement of that period gone the round with the excise officer, and expressed his determination to banish any transgressor from the Island'.

By the late nineteenth century, the full protection of the law extended even to the humblest Colonsay cottager. In its issue for 29 November 1873, the *Argyllshire Herald* carried a lengthy report of a court case which had been tried at Inveraray on 21 November. It involved Commander Duncan Stewart, formerly of the Royal Navy, who was married to Ferooza, daughter of Sir John McNeill, the diplomat. She had died in 1871.

Stewart was charged with 'assaulting a widow named Margaret or Peggy McPhee or McNeill, on the public road near Kiloran House'. According to the indictment, it was alleged:

> that on the 16th June 1873, the defendant did violently seize hold of the woman McNeill by the wrist and elbow of the right hand, and twist it behind her back, did struggle with and push or throw her backwards upon the ground, and did forcibly pull or drag her for a distance of fifty yards or thereby along the road, and did at the same time threaten to lock or imprison her

in a cellar at Kiloran House, by all of which she was wounded and bruised to the serious injury of her person, and was put in a great state of terror and alarm for her personal safety.

The case aroused great interest in Argyll 'on account of the social position of the parties concerned'. Peggy McPhee (McNeill would have been her married name), is described as 'a poor-looking woman of about 50 years'. She gave evidence that she was on the way to 'Kiloran House' from her own house at 'Reasagbuie' for the purpose of delivering two pairs of stockings which she had knitted. On her way home she was intercepted by Commander Stewart, who demanded to know what she was up to, and found her in possession of 'some meal and a bottle of sour milk'. She was manhandled and bullied as described in the indictment, and on being allowed home, 'took to bed that night and did not rise for ten weeks'.

The cross-examination of Peggy McPhee was somewhat farcical, as she was a native Gaelic speaker not fluent in English. From the court reporter's point of view 'great difficulty was experienced in getting the witness to answer the questions put. After giving every conceivable reply but the one required, she generally took refuge in Gaelic'.

In his defence Duncan Stewart claimed the woman had no right to be on the road, and that he had used reasonable force in apprehending her. He claimed that 'a system of pilfering was being practised at his home farm', and that he had taken the opportunity to challenge the widow McNeill. When eventually he had ascertained what she was carrying in her bundle, he let her go.

The minister, the Rev Donald McLean, went to see 'the woman McNeill' after the incident. She complained of stiffness in her right arm, which Stewart admitted he had twisted behind her back 'in the mode practised by policemen'. McLean testified that on leaving he offered Peggy a shilling to buy some medicine, and 'he noticed that she held out her hand to receive the shilling quite freely'. His impression was that 'the woman was exaggerating her injury, if not shamming'.

Finally, Dr McIndo, from Islay, was called (as a Crown witness) to say that on examination he had failed to find any indications that she had been assaulted in any way, or any trace of a swelling. Considering this examination took place 'six or seven weeks after the alleged assault', these observations were hardly surprising.

Mr James Adam, the advocate appearing for Stewart, maintained that the *locus* of the assault had not been proved, 'because the road on which the alleged assault was said to have been committed, was not the only road between Kiloran farm steading and Scalasaig Inn, and that no proper indication was given to show which of the two was meant'.

On this technicality, the Sheriff-Substitute of Argyllshire, Sir George Home, Bart, directed the jury to return a verdict of not guilty, which they duly did. This 'trial' had lasted nearly eight hours. According to the *Argyllshire Herald*, 'Commander Stewart was loudly cheered on leaving the Court'.

In 1989, in a not dissimilar case, an industrial tribunal found a Highland laird had subjected an employee to 'humiliating and upsetting attacks, delivered in a bullying and intimidating manner'. The victim, who was awarded substantial compensation for loss of earnings, was reported to have said that he believed justice had been done, 'having felt in his last two years in the job that he was back in feudal days when a laird's word was law, whether it be right or wrong'.

Or Victorian days? Further comment is superfluous!

FERRIES

As in neighbouring islands, the advent of postal services provided the basis for the development of regular sailings to Colonsay. A sub-post office was established in 1871, after representations by Lord Colonsay. It was a sub-office under

Greenock, as from thence the steamer *Dunvegan Castle* set off for its voyages to the Hebrides. In 1875 the *Dunara Castle* took over the service.

Mrs Frances Murray, an intrepid lady who spent the summers at Oronsay House with her family between 1880 and 1887, has some interesting descriptive passages of life in the Hebrides at that time, which were published in her book *Summer in the Hebrides*. She had been attracted to the island 'by the high-sounding advertisement in a well-known time-table' where she read that:

> . . . a run to this island will be the happiest recollection in a man's terrestrial career; for there is the purest atmos-phere, and the mildest climate in the west of Scotland. Its scenery is beautiful and varied: its grand gigantic cliffs, in front of which the seagulls, cormorants, and eider ducks, float and scream continually in countless thousands: its pure yellow sandy beaches, some a mile wide, on which the never-ceasing Atlantic swell tumbles in and expends itself in white foam: its endless and extensive caves, are sights that should be seen!

Mrs Murray had to admit that 'fervid as its language was, we were not disappointed in the reality'.

But in her day the ferry services were not always very punctual or reliable – 'a boat may advertise to leave at seven in the evening, and yet keep you waiting till seven in the morning, without any manner of apology'. It was particu-larly inconvenient for the Murray family; as their holiday house was on Oronsay, they often had to set out several hours before the advertised departure time in order to cross the Strand safely. Frequently the family had to spend most of the night at the pier at Scalasaig, in a store house, though they also spent 'many a pleasant hour in the inn', waiting 'for the hoarse whistle which signalled the ferrymen to hasten to get all aboard the boat'.

The ferry boat was loaded with 'bundles, babies, bales

and beasts', and made its way out to the steamer. Often every available inch was occupied by men and boys, and 'barrels and boxes, baskets and bundles of all kinds and sizes tumbled into the boat as she rose and fell in the surge'.

In the 1880s the 'Islay packet' was a boat of 15 tons, heavy enough to ferry cattle, which sailed to Islay once a week to bring over letters and passengers.

Mrs Murray travelled on the SS *Dunara Castle*, which was owned by McCallum, Orme and Co Ltd. There were deck cabins, state rooms, ladies' cabins, and a saloon. The company advertised that 'a Stewardess is always in attendance, and special attention is paid to ladies travelling alone'. From 1881 the *Dunara Castle* alternated with the steamer *Hebridean*, and after 1898, with the *Hebrides*, in the summer months. These vessels ran circular tours from Glasgow lasting from 7 to 8 days, departing from berth no 44 at the Lancefield Quay in Glasgow every 10 days or so. A cabin for the round trip cost £9. There were occasional special cruises to St Kilda, Loch Roag, Loch Scavaig and round the Isle of Skye.

These two steamers ran throughout the 1920s and 1930s and are still fondly remembered by many older residents and visitors. The *Dunara Castle*, for example, served the Western Isles from 1875 to 1948. They were well-appointed steamers with good accommodation, 'lighted by electricity' and with what the company described in uncharacteristically imaginative language, 'first class *cruisine*'!

These vessels were a lifeline for the islands, providing a regular service for passengers and freight, to and from Glasgow. This can be seen from a typical itinerary for SS *Hebrides* in the 1930s: Glasgow – Greenock – Port Askaig – Colonsay – Oban – Tobermory – Coll – Tiree – Castlebay (Barra) – Lochboisdale – Loch Skipport – Lochmaddy – Scalpay – Tarbert – Uig – Dunvegan – Loch Pooltiel – Portnalong – Carbost – Tiree, returning to Glasgow by way of Colonsay and Islay.

In 1948 McCallum Orme was absorbed by MacBrayne's,

and Colonsay was serviced by the TSS *Lochness*, which operated a special excursion from Oban to Colonsay in the 1949 season only. Thereafter she worked the Inner Isles route, with extra trips between Oban and Colonsay. Meanwhile, in April 1949 MacBrayne's *Lochiel* started to service Colonsay, its West Loch Tarbert to Port Askaig run extending to Scalasaig twice a week in winter and four times a week in summer. The *Lochiel* was superseded by the *Arran*, which served the 'four islands' run: Islay–Jura–Colonsay–Gigha. This service ended in 1972, when the Inner Isles steamer *Claymore* made special sailings to Colonsay from Oban.

In 1965 a new pier was built at Scalasaig, at a cost of £159,000, replacing the quay built in 1867. Five years later a car ferry started serving Colonsay. Until then motor vehicles were rare. Indeed, at one time, they were banned. An estate worker who announced his intention to purchase a motor bike to get to and from his work was told that, while there was nothing to prevent him doing this, he might find that he no longer had a job to go to.

From 1973 Scalasaig was served by a car ferry from Oban, three times a week. Normally the vessel used was the *Columba*, with a capacity of 35 cars and 600 passengers and 26 crew in summer. In winter it was licensed to carry a maximum of 400 passengers and 24 crew.

By contrast, when the *Columba* was finally retired in 1988, to become a luxury Hebridean cruise ship, the new car ferry, the 2,500-ton *Isle of Mull*, could carry 80 cars and 1,000 passengers. There were considerable problems with the new ship. First of all it was discovered to be overweight, and various fittings were replaced by plastic equivalents. Then it was found that the shipbuilders had made an error during construction, and the new ferry had to be taken out of service to have its length extended.

Calmac brought the *Isle of Mull* out to Colonsay for the islanders to see, and at one time almost the total population of the islands was on board the new ferry. One islander remembered that it suddenly crossed her mind that if the ship sailed away then the island would be deserted and that it might be a NIREX plot to clear the islands for a nuclear dump!

A new 90m (295ft) concrete pier was built for the new RO-RO (roll-on-roll-off) ferries alongside the old pier. Most of the island turned out in 1988 to see Britain's largest floating crane, the 250-ton capacity *Mersey Mammoth*, lift the 36m (118ft) long prefabricated steel beam end ramp into position. The hinged ramp can be raised or lowered by up to 5m (16½ft), allowing the new ferry to berth at any state of tide. The new facilities cost £1.5 million pounds.

The changeover to the new service was not accomplished smoothly. New pier office and facilities were built, but there were delays, and a certain lack of sympathy from Calmac about the inconvenience of having to house foot passengers and their luggage in an incomplete structure covered with sheep droppings.

The new service proved to be immensely complicated, and not at all convenient for the islanders or their visitors. It was announced that because the car deck was completely enclosed, the *Isle of Mull* could not carry the tankers that brought petrol and diesel to Colonsay, or any dangerous chemicals or explosives, which also ruled out some agricultural cargo, in the form of insecticides and fertilisers. In addition, livestock could no longer be carried loose, but would have to be loaded on to floats while on board ship. When an older relief ship was being operated, this was not a problem.

The timetable itself was extremely variable, and not at all geared to hotel or self-catering visitors, who were faced with sitting up all night in 'aircraft' type seats – unlike the *Columba*, the new ferry had no cabins for passengers. An extra service was introduced, using the Islay ferry. Once a week, on a Wednesday, the *Iona* left Kennacraig in Kintyre, calling at Port Askaig on Islay, proceeding to Scalasaig in Colonsay, then on to Oban, returning to Kennacraig by the same route later that day. For the first time it became possible to make a day trip to Colonsay, as this new service allowed passengers six hours ashore while the ferry made its way to Oban and back.

TELEPHONE

The telegraph was introduced to Colonsay in 1895. Two years later the TS *Monarch* laid a new cable, and Sir John McNeill had the first telephones installed, linking the post office in Scalasaig to the hotel and Colonsay House.

An automatic telephone exchange was installed on Colonsay in 1970, at a cost of £68,000. Since this meant the permanent loss of the full time job of telephone operator, islanders were not sure that this was an improvement.

The Colonsay Hotel produces a local telephone directory: measuring three inches by four (7.6 × 10cm), it contains a grand total of 57 entries. The 'Non-Yellow Pages' on the back cover lists 30 numbers, covering a range of services from Rent-a-Boat and Bicycle Hire to the Coastguard and Insemination (artificial)!

The futuristic contrivances on the hill behind the hotel at Scalasaig are there to relay telephone signals to and from the mainland.

MEDICAL SERVICES

There has been a resident doctor on Colonsay since 1897. Before that, it was not a healthy place to live. Death statistics for the period 1855–91 show that 25 per cent of deaths were aged 0–19, while 12 per cent of deaths were between the ages of 20 and 29. These were mostly caused by respiratory ailments: tuberculosis, asthma, bronchitis and pneumonia. Just over 10 per cent of the deaths were infants between 0 and 1.

Today there is a district nurse as well as a doctor, who occupy a small surgery at Scalasaig. There is an island ambulance service. In dire emergencies, evacuation by rescue helicopter can be arranged. In other circumstances patients are sent by ferry to Oban, where there is a full range of hospital and medical services. A dentist visits Colonsay at regular intervals.

Although he never practised on his native island, one of Colonsay's most famous sons was a medical man. Dr Roger McNeill was the Medical Officer of Health for the county of Argyll from 1890 until his death in 1924. After his student years at the university of Edinburgh he spent some years in private practice and world travel, before returning to London where he was in charge of two hospital ships stationed in the Thames during the great smallpox epidemic of the early 1880s. In 1883 he became resident medical officer in Gesto Hospital in the Isle of Skye, from where he moved to Argyll in 1890.

In his later years he used to visit Colonsay every year, and he is buried at Kilchattan. He was highly regarded both on his native island and in the medical profession.

POPULATION

There has been compulsory registration of births, marriages and deaths in Scotland only since 1855, so information and statistics for the period before that are sketchy and often unreliable. Colonsay was constituted as a separate registration district, and Neil MacMillan, schoolmaster, was appointed registrar.

In the decennial census organised in 1841 by Alexander McNeill, the parochial schoolmaster, assisted by his son Daniel, it was found that the total population was 979, which is the highest figure recorded for Colonsay and Oronsay. Since then the population has declined unrelentingly. There was a drastic drop during the second half of the nineteenth century, and thereafter a steady decline, which continues to the present day. In the period 1841–91 the population declined from the maximum of 979 to only 381 – only 39 per cent of what it had been. In 1891 the islands had 50 per cent fewer surnames than in 1841; the McNeills increased from 13 per cent in 1841, to 24 per cent in 1891. By 1951 the population had dropped to 233. In 1961 it was 166 and in 1971, 137. The population at the 1981 census was also 137, but that marked a slight recovery from the low point of 127 reported by a researcher in 1977. An unofficial 'head count' in 1989 suggested that by the 1991 census the population will have dropped below 120.

When visiting Colonsay in 1836, Lord Teignmouth offered some thoughts as to the sufficiency of the population, which was then about 900. He thought it was 'insufficient for the labour required – it has been too much thinned by emigrations to America, about ten and three years ago' – that is, in the early 1820s. He added: 'it is found necessary to supply the deficiency of hands by labourers from Islay and Jura. The emigrants, by the last accounts, were desirous of returning to their native islands'. Only ten years after this was written, the mass emigrations of the mid-nineteenth century were in full swing.

The population of the islands at various times can be summarised in the following table, which is compiled from various sources:

1755	439	1891	381
1772	550	1901	313
1792	718	1911	273
1801	805	1921	282
1811	786	1931	238
1821	904	1951	233
1831	893	1961	166
1841	979	1971	137
1851	837	1977	127
1861	598	1981	137
1871	456	1989	122
1881	397		

A detailed study of the population in 1977 by John W.

Sheets of the Department of Sociology and Anthropology at Central Missouri State University, Warrensburg, Missouri, gives a breakdown of the population structure, analysed by age, sex and origin. He found that Colonsay had higher population fertility, a shorter generation length, and a longer female reproductive span, than the neighbouring island of Jura. He divides the population into 'natives' and 'migrants', where natives are defined as having at least one parent born on Colonsay:

Age	1977	Native			Migrant		
		M	F	Total	M	F	Total
50–90	44	15	16	31	4	9	13
20–49	45	13	10	23	11	11	22
0–19	38	13	14	27	5	6	11
	127			81 (63%)			46 (37%)

Sheets found that 45 of the natives (55 per cent) had either McNeill or MacPhee ancestry, so although only a handful of people bear these names today, there are still many familial connections. Of the 'migrants', Sheets found that 7 came from other parts of the Hebrides, 22 from the rest of Scotland (including 12 from Glasgow), and 17 from England.

EMPLOYMENT

A cut-back of the number of workers employed on Colonsay Estate in 1970 caused problems, and some emigration, but was considered necessary to make the estate economically viable. The island of Oronsay was sold in 1978 to Adam Bergius, of Teacher's whisky, reportedly for £100,000. In 1983 it changed hands again. It was bought by an American, Ike Colburn, who proceeded to spend a lot of money and employ a lot of labour in improving Oronsay House and converting many of the farm buildings to self-catering accommodation. At the moment a family is employed to manage the complex, and another couple have the tenancy of the island as a sheep farm.

It is unusual for anybody on Colonsay to have just one job. Most of the active, adult population, male and female, have more than one way of making a living, working a few hours each week in different jobs, which may vary according to the time of year. The hotel is a major employer, needing bar staff, waitresses, kitchen staff, and cleaners for the never-ending task of preparing its rooms and chalets for the next ferry. Colonsay Estate needs people to make its holiday cottages and flats ready for visitors.

The local farmers have to be able to turn their hand to a whole range of skills – basically anything that breaks down on the island is repaired there. If spare parts have to be ordered from the mainland, it needs considerable descriptive skill to ensure that the correct bits and pieces are supplied.

There are a few trained tradesmen on the island who can cope with most building and construction jobs. With the modernisation of holiday cottages and the advent of electricity there has been quite a lot of small-scale building work over the last few years, with one or two larger projects. Sometimes firms from Oban are brought over to provide specialist services.

There is a little casual work available to support the few able-bodied residents who do not have their own farm or enterprise. Farmers always need help with fencing, sheep dipping, or any of the thousand and one things that need doing on a working farm, and of course they need somebody to look after things when they are off the island. The Site of Special Scientific Interest at Balnahard requires local monitoring and management on behalf of the Nature Conservancy, and this provides a little part-time employment throughout the year. A few people are showing signs of exploiting the tourist market – something which so far has not been done to any great extent, outside the accommodation field. Certainly there is scope for imaginative marketing, bearing in mind that the kind of tourists coming to Colonsay and Oronsay are definitely at the better-educated and more affluent end of the market.

TOURISM

The development of tourism as a local industry is something which is new to Colonsay and Oronsay. Tourists have been coming to the islands since the eighteenth century, but it is really only since 1979 that the islands have been advertised as an up-market tourist destination.

The proprietors of the Isle of Colonsay Hotel have been very much to the fore in this respect. Typically, island hotels in Scotland were old-fashioned, cold, draughty and uncomfortable, with an uninspiring menu and a range of alcoholic beverages limited to beer and the local malt whiskies. In the days when the island visitors tended to be interested in the traditional outdoor pursuits of hunting, shooting and fishing, perhaps the expectation of being cold, wet and miserable was part of the appeal. A dram or two in the evening around a peat fire in the hotel bar probably made the misery acceptable.

But these days are gone. Today's visitors require comfort, warmth and good food, and are prepared to pay for them. To be sure, a holiday on Colonsay and Oronsay is still very much an outdoor experience, but people are more interested now in photographing wildlife or observing it through binoculars than in obliterating it. Through books and television, visitors are aware of history and archaeology, and want to visit the interesting range of island sites. Town dwellers want information on sea shells and plant life, and come ready to study and to learn.

The Isle of Colonsay Hotel has shown what is possible in the way of providing superlative accommodation in a small 'family' hotel. The *Good Hotel Guide* credits the proprietors with 'endless perfectionist energy'. Their bookings suggest that this is what people want, and that their customers are satisfied, because return visits are a major feature of their business.

There has been an inn at Scalasaig since the eighteenth century. It is likely that the same architect was responsible for the church, school, inn, and adjoining small building – they are all very much in the same style. From the County Valuation Rolls we learn that the innkeeper in 1841 was Peggy Martin, who looked after her five children as well as the inn. In February 1844 she was credited with running 'a small but neat inn'. By 1851 it was in the charge of John and Peggy Bell, both natives of Colonsay, and by 1861 it was run by Margaret Bell on her own. At this time it had '10 rooms with windows'. Subsequently Donald McNeill had the inn, for over twenty years. In 1883 a Miss McNeill at the hotel was described as 'very attentive'.

The earliest record of ratable value is for 1890/91, when it was £18! Thereafter it was run until the 1920s by three sisters: Catherine, Flora and Margaret McNeill. The last two later married, and became known as Flora McAlpin and Margaret Black. They were succeeded by David Clark, who ran the hotel until the 1950s, and then by Mr and Mrs Jones. The present proprietors, Kevin and Christa Byrne, came to Colonsay in 1978.

Although the tourist season is still only 5 to 6 months long, it is getting longer all the time. People in the tourist industry are beginning to realise the potential for marketing island holidays in the autumn and winter months, when the bird life is so much more interesting and the archaeology so much easier to see in the absence of bracken and long grass. Undoubtedly there is a good living to be made – not in exploiting tourists but in providing them with the range of goods and services which will make them appreciate their island holiday more – and ensure their return.

The latest available figures for ferry traffic show a marked increase during the 1980s. In 1982, 7,229 passengers and 1,128 cars were transported to Colonsay; by 1988 this had risen to over 13,000 passengers and 2,300 cars. As the Laird does not allow holiday caravans on to the island, and as camping is forbidden (except for educational groups), the island is now at saturation point in the summer season. There is probably accommodation on the island for 250 people, including the hotel and its chalets, the Colonsay House holiday flats, Colonsay Estate self-catering cottages, and private houses rented out to visitors. So, it is unlikely that the number of cars coming to Colonsay will increase as dramatically in the 1990s.

One resident philosopher even sees the AIDS epidemic as working to Colonsay's advantage! According to this line of analysis, domestic tranquillity and family holidays are now a safer and more appealing prospect than the sun, surf and permissiveness of foreign holidays. Perhaps there is indeed a change in our national holiday habits, which will benefit tourism in Argyll and the islands.

The limited amount of accommodation available means that Colonsay and Oronsay will never become overwhelmed by visitors. Even at the height of the summer season it is amazing how the increased population is absorbed. Although the islands are small, they are large enough to take the extra numbers. Although the population is trebled at the height of the season, this is still just within the bounds of acceptability, and a great boon to the islands' economy.

There is a danger that the product could be destroyed by insensitive development or over-ambitious projects. Thus, these islands are probably not a suitable location for a massive, luxury, leisure development bringing hundreds of jet-setters to golf courses and heated swimming pools. For one thing, the infrastructure to support such a scheme does not exist, while it would certainly destroy the island atmosphere that attracts people at the moment.

Equally, a caravan park on Colonsay would be disastrous. Under the present management it is not a possibility, but it is devoutly to be hoped that the planning authorities will veto any such proposal at any time in the future. On the other hand, a sensitively designed complex of purpose-built holiday chalets would release today's self-catering cottages back into the local housing market, and would be more suitable for visitors. The cottages now used as holiday homes were built and intended for permanent occupation, and really need to be lived in throughout the year. Otherwise, they begin to suffer from damp and develop all sorts of structural problems.

HOUSING

There is a desperate shortage of suitable housing for local people on Colonsay, which is a matter of serious social concern. There are no immediate proposals to remedy the situation. The island Community Council is taking the lead in trying to provide a forum in which all the island's interests can be represented. Undoubtedly the island's future is, for better or worse, intimately bound up with the future of Colonsay Estate. It is unrealistic to expect one family to shoulder the burden for the whole community, not to mention undemocratic, and the somewhat paternalistic attitude of the Strathconas and McNeills before them will assuredly not last for ever.

The present Lord Strathcona has the interests of the islands at heart, but is trying to run his self-catering enterprise as a profit-making business, or at least one which will pay its own way. He can no longer afford the financial generosity of his predecessors, who effectively subsidised the island out of their own pockets for sixty years. Inevitably this brings him into conflict with some islanders where there is a clash of interests. There is no reason to suspect that he or his heirs will ever succumb to the temptation to put the profit motive above all social considerations, but the present balance is unsatisfactory and now is the time for islanders to make their views known.

Although Colonsay Estate is running profitably at the moment, it has been on the market in the past. Inevitably, therefore, there is some talk on the island about alternatives.

It could become the island retreat of a wealthy pop star, which would probably have the effect of releasing some of the cottages back into the housing market. Or, it could become a luxury country house hotel, echoing the success of the present hotel, but on a larger and grander scale. This would, of course, entail extensive and expensive conversion costs. Perhaps some group or organisation would buy it and use it as a retreat and conference centre, or for educational purposes.

Colonsay has faced housing problems before. The deserted settlement at Riasg Buidhe was abandoned only in the early 1920s, when the population were re-housed at Glassard, on the outskirts of Scalasaig. The old houses had earth floors and thatched roofs. One room would have had a few beds in it, and the loft would have been spread with bracken and twigs for the children.

According to the 1986 Valuation Roll, Lord Strathcona owns no fewer than 34 properties on Colonsay, including self-catering units. Argyll and Bute District Council has 5 council houses and 21 properties are privately owned. Some of these are holiday homes, occupied for only a few weeks each year. The schoolhouse, the manse, and the doctor's house are owned by Strathclyde Regional Council, the Church of Scotland, and Argyll and Clyde Health Board.

Perhaps it is idle to speculate on such matters where there is no immediate threat – 'sufficient unto the day is the evil thereof'. But experiences in similar locations in Scotland suggest that local inhabitants should at the very least keep themselves informed on such matters.

OYSTER FARM

An outstanding example of innovative enterprise which has not yet reached its full marketing potential is the oyster and mussel farm located at the Strand. These tidal waters are ideal for the purpose. Apart from the ease of access, their main advantage is their isolation. Oysters are very sensitive to pollution, which is one aspect of modern life thankfully absent from these remote islands.

The species of oyster that is farmed at the Strand comes from Japanese waters. Unlike our native British oyster, it will not spawn until the water temperature reaches 21–22°C (69–70°F) – which is not likely. The Colonsay oysters therefore grow steadily for the three years that it takes for them to reach maturity, and can be harvested at any time of the year. The oyster 'seed' is bought in from the Channel Islands, and 'planted' in the sea between Colonsay and Oronsay. Quite a lot of management is involved, which because of the tides can only take place for about fourteen days out of every month. As the oysters mature, they are moved to different cages and to different positions, until at last they are ready for harvesting.

Before they are removed from the sea and sent to the best hotels and restaurants in Glasgow, Edinburgh and London, the oysters have to be 'trained'. In their natural environment, the shell is open for feeding most of the time, so the muscle that holds the shell closed is not naturally equipped with great strength and endurance. This is achieved by moving the oysters nearer the shore, so that they are exposed for increasingly longer periods at low tide. By the time they are harvested, their tiny muscles have the capacity to hold the shells tightly shut for several days, thus ensuring that they reach their markets in good condition.

It is therefore quite possible for visitors to take oysters home with them, thus prolonging their island experience for a little longer. They can also be purchased on the island.

FISHING

Lobsters, prawns and crabs are caught locally by small, inshore fishing boats. There is a ready market in season at the hotel, and with self-catering visitors, or the catches can be marketed at Oban.

Gone are the days when almost every islander was a

crofter/fisherman who supported himself and his family by his own efforts by harvesting the crops of both land and sea. Although the old ways still persist, with the advent of electricity it has become possible to stock freezers with the same range of frozen produce available to the mainlanders. Any visit to the mainland will inevitably end with a trip to an Oban supermarket to stock up with what have become the 'necessities' of modern life.

ELECTRICITY

Mains electricity came to Colonsay and Oronsay only in 1983, and was celebrated by a ceremony in the hotel in that October. Apart from consumer appliances and chest freezers, one of the major ways in which this has affected the islands is in the arrival of electric fences, which are now everywhere. A side-effect of this has been the recovery of roadside habitats for plants and birds in some parts of the island, as sheep are now confined to fields and hills, where formerly they wandered freely.

Most of the electric fences on the island run off mains electricity, and *not* off batteries, and can give a *very* nasty jolt! In view of the fact that they are a relatively recent phenomenon, which might come as a surprise to previous visitors, and also because they are *not* always as clearly marked as they might be, it is worth emphasising that they are *extremely dangerous*.

The conservation area at Balnahard is entirely surrounded by electric fencing, and stiles are provided at what. are thought to be logical crossing points. But these are not really sufficiently sturdy or adequate, nor sufficiently numerous, so take care.

NUCLEAR WASTE

In a glossy discussion document published in 1987, NIREX (the Nuclear Industry Radioactive Waste Executive) considered various options for disposing of nuclear waste. As this coincided with the expenditure of £1.5 million for the new pier facilities – £12,000 for every man, woman and child on the island – some islanders became suspicious of Scottish Office and EEC benevolence and looked for alternative explanations.

At one time the Cruise Missile option achieved some popularity, as Colonsay would be an excellent place to hide mobile weapons systems, and existing harbour facilities were not suitable. But international developments seemed to rule that out as a reason – unless as some argued, the sheer inertial force of lumbering governmental bureaucracy just could not be stopped in time. When the NIREX brochure, *The Way Forward*, showed Colonsay as having a 'geological environment considered to have potential for repository development', some islanders were sure this was the real reason for the new pier.

However, announcements by NIREX in 1989 seemed to indicate that the two areas under consideration for the disposal of nuclear waste were in Cumbria and in Caithness, so the bar-room philosophers of Scalasaig are scratching their heads, searching for other explanations for their new pier.

10   GAELIC LIFE AND CULTURE

The islands of Colonsay and Oronsay are part of a seriously threatened cultural province in which Gaelic language, music and folklore barely survive. Gaelic is still the language of everyday communication amongst the older folk in the islands, but their children and grandchildren have abandoned it in favour of English, which is more than a little sad but apparently inevitable, given the pressures of the media and pop cultures of late twentieth-century Britain and the almost total lack of effective government policies aimed at counteracting prevailing trends.

Gaels started to come into the territory of what is now called Scotland before AD300. Settling first of all in what is now Argyll, Gaelic-speaking people gradually spread their culture outwards from their cultural heartland, westwards and north to the Outer Hebrides, Lochaber, Skye, Lochalsh and Sutherland, and eastwards to Galloway, Central Scotland, Perthshire, then onward to Moray and Buchan.

In the middle of the ninth century a direct descendant of the first kings of Dalriada married the heiress to the matrilineal Pictish kingdom and so Kenneth MacAlpin became the first ruler of the united kingdoms of the Picts and the Scots – the basis of modern Scotland.

But it was just at this time that Viking raiders were making their first forays into the Western Isles. From AD800 until AD1156, the Gaelic-speaking Western Isles and much of the adjacent mainland were totally under Norse domination. Political allegiance was to the Norwegian king, while the ecclesiastical capital of the diocese of Sodor and Man was Trondheim. More significantly, large areas of Scotland were occupied by Norse settlers, especially the northern archipelagos of Shetland and Orkney, the mainland districts of Caithness and Sutherland, the Outer Hebrides, and the island of Islay. These areas were densely settled by farming folk of Norse origin, who intermarried over the centuries with the local Gaelic population and were eventually absorbed, though the hundreds of surviving place-names preserve the extent of their influence.

We have already seen (in chapter 5) how the half-Gael, half-Norse war leader, Somerled successfully defeated Olaf through a combination of brilliant guerrilla warfare and revolutionary naval tactics. His successors gradually built up the power, influence and extent of what became known as the Lordship of the Isles. When, in AD1263 King Haakon of Norway was unsuccessful in reasserting Norse power in a campaign which ended at the Battle of Largs, the way was clear in the west for Clan Donald to become very powerful indeed – and in the end too powerful, posing too great a threat to the stability of the emerging Scottish nation state.

FOLKLORE

Much of the surviving folklore of the Hebrides has to be seen in the context of these events. The idea that the Lords of the Isles could somehow recapture the 'Golden Age' of Finn MacCoul and Deirdre and all the other heroes and heroines of Gaelic culture is always just below the surface of daily life. Many of the tales and legends which are recounted as if they were historical events that really happened, are in fact common Indo-European folk stories adapted to local circumstances. Whether this makes them more or less real is a matter for each individual. There is no single objective answer, for reality changes for each person, and Hebridean reality is very different from urban reality.

For one thing, the dead are far more 'present' in everyday life in the islands. Indeed, the ancestors are part of the living reality of the present. This is something which is difficult for visitors and incomers to grasp, but which, after a while, seems so obvious that it no longer requires to be stated.

The Scots writer Neil Munro has written movingly of these dilemmas, particularly in his intriguing novel, *The Well at the World's End*. In this book, questions of reality and illusion, past and present, individual and community are explored from within the culture. He shows convincingly the depths of cultural conditioning which transcend generations, leaving us in no doubt that there is an underlying reality ever present in the landscape, part of the psychic geography of every native Scot. A few incomers have proved that this reality can be penetrated and learned by those who can read the right cultural maps.

IAIN OG ILE

John Francis Campbell of Islay, always known in Celtic circles as Iain Og Ile, was the first to bridge the two cultures, Gaelic and English, and interpret them to each other. His four volumes of *Popular Tales of the West Highlands*, published from 1860 to 1862, contain the results of years of recording local stories, written down in Gaelic and transcribed into English. In almost all cases, when Campbell and his co-workers wrote these stories down, it was the first time in their long history that they had been committed to paper, having been passed down by word of mouth for untold generations.

One of Campbell's stories is about the Witch or Wise Woman of Jura and MacPhie of Colonsay. There was a Caileach (old woman) in Jura who had a magic ball of thread by means of which she could draw any person or thing towards her. MacPhie was in her clutches, and was not allowed to leave Jura. On several occasions he tried to escape to his native Colonsay in his boat, but always the Caileach would spot him, throw the magic ball of thread into his boat, and so bring him back to shore.

Eventually MacPhie pretended to be content with his bondage, and found out that the magic of the Caileach's thread could only be broken if it was cut by an equally magic hatchet. Early one morning MacPhie crept away, with the hatchet, and made his escape from Jura in a small boat. When the Caileach noticed his absence, she rushed as usual to the top of Beinn a Chaolis, and hailed MacPhie:

A Mhic a Phie
A Ghaoils' thasgaidh
An d' fhag thu air a chladach mi?

Oh, MacPhie
My love and treasure
Have you left me on the strand?

She hurled the magic ball of thread into MacPhie's boat, but he cut it with the Caileach's hatchet and made his escape. She was distraught:

A Mhic a Phie
Charrich, granda
'An d' fhag thu air a chladach mi?

Oh, MacPhie
Rough-skinned and foul
Have you left me on the strand?

In despair she slid down the mountain to the sea shore, pleading with MacPhie to return. But he would not, and the marks left by the old woman's heels as she slid down Beinn a Chaolis can still be seen. They are called Sgriob na Cailich – the slide of the old woman. They start near the top of the hill as rocky ravines and end in a trail of boulder scree.

This kind of mythology will be familiar to those brought up on the exploits of Greek and Roman gods. In a pre-scientific age, natural features and natural phenomena were often explained in this way. But since the stories address some of the most basic tribulations of the human condition, who are we to devalue them by asking awkward questions about their reality or historicity? Such questions are irrelevant and miss the point.

In the case of the Witch of Jura the story highlights the dilemma of an ageing woman who thinks that she has her man for life, while he has secretly been longing for years to escape from the relationship, without knowing how this can be done. Finally he 'cuts the thread' leaving the relationship, and in this case his long-time mate, literally and symbolically 'washed up' on the shore of the ocean of life.

Truly there are many layers to these stories, and how much more meaningful they are when the teller can point to the scars on the mountainside left by the Caileach's heels.

One of Iain Og Ile's many informants was John MacGilvray, described as a 'labourer' from 'Baille Raomainn, Colonsay'. When Campbell recorded his version of 'The Knight of the Red Shield' in 1860 John MacGilvray was 72 years old. His father was Farquar MacGilvray, a native of Mull, who had learned the story there in his boyhood. Farquar served in the army in North America for seven years, and subsequently settled in Colonsay. He died around 1820, aged about 75. Assuming he memorised the story in his childhood, as did his son John, this takes the story back to the 1750s, and doubtless it was passed on from generation to generation for many hundreds of years before that. What is remarkable, at least by today's standards, is that the story as written down by Campbell consists of thirteen solid pages of type in *Popular Tales* – an astounding feat of memory repeated many, many times in the pages of Campbell's tomes.

DONALD MACKINNON

In the same tradition of informed scholarship was Donald MacKinnon of Colonsay (1839–1914), the first Professor of Celtic in Edinburgh University – an honour which many in 1882 felt should have gone to John Francis Campbell.

MacKinnon's wife was Catherine MacPhee (1842–1917). Their daughters Catherine and Mary died in 1949 and 1960. All this is recorded on a suitably Celtic gravestone in Kilchattan burial ground. Colonsay has produced many men and women who have left their mark on the wider world, but Donald MacKinnon must surely have a good claim for having done the most to support and promote his native culture.

Professor MacKinnon has left us a very interesting account of life in Colonsay, going back to the potato failure of 1846. He reckons that of all the people who lived in Lower Kilchattan in his boyhood, all except his own family emigrated to Canada around 1852. He records that the staple foods were potatoes, rabbits and mutton. Considerable quantities of flounders, plaice and saithe were caught and salted for winter use, along with some sand-eels. Cod and ling were mostly exported. Seals weere killed for their oil, which was used for greasing wool. The skin made excellent tobacco pouches, but MacKinnon had never heard of seal-flesh being eaten. The people ate lots of shellfish, especially whelks and limpets, though cockles, lobsters and crabs were also eaten, especially after very low ebb tides.

In winter, cottages were lit by dip-candles or by oil extracted from saithe-liver, and burnt in the old-fashioned *cruisgean* or cruisie, with a wick taken from the common rush.

Bread loaves were unheard of, though flour-meal was common in the Big House, and rare in the cottages. A farm labourer could be hired for £5 a year, or a girl for £2. Unskilled labour was rewarded by a wage of a shilling a day without food, or eightpence if meals were provided. Milk and its products – butter, cheese, curds and cream – were an important part of the local diet. MacKinnon's account has particular value since it is by a native islander. In later life he lived at Balnahard, where he heightened the ceilings and raised the roof in order to make it into a commodious residence more fitted to a Victorian professor. It was he who is said to have referred to

Gaelic as the language spoken in the Garden of Eden.

CUSTOMS

In 1716 Martin Martin mentions that there was 'a modern Crucifix' on the altar of the church at Oronsay, and that the most valuable of several precious stones from this ornamental crucifix was 'in the custody of *Mack-Duffie*, in black *Raimused* Village, and it is us'd as a *Catholicon* for Diseases'.

Martin visited Oronsay, and recorded a local custom of walking around the church there 'sunways', ie clockwise, before entering. As to burial customs, he says:

> About a quarter of a Mile on the South-side of the Church there is a Carne, in which there is a Stone Cross fix'd, call'd *Mack-Duffie's Cross*; for when any of the Heads of this Family were to be interr'd, their Corps was laid on this Cross for some moments, in their way towards the Church.

A description of one of the Oronsay grave-slabs is worth repeating:

> there is a Ship under Sail, and a two-handed Sword engraven on the principal Tombstone, and this Inscription, *Hic jacit Malcolumbus Mac-Duffie de Collonsay*; his Coat of Arms and Colour-Staff is fix'd in a Stone, thro which a Hole is made to hold it.

While he was staying in Colonsay, at the inn which is now the hotel, his illiterate landlord asked to borrow his Book, (ie his Bible) which he used to fan the face of a sick member of his family, morning and night. It transpired that there was 'an antient Custom of fanning the Face of the Sick with the Leaves of the Bible'.

Only a brief description of the landscape is given by Martin. He mentions the brown and sandy coastal soil, producing little although ploughed three times a year, and he describes the interior of the island as 'rocky and heathy', with most places 'prettily mingled with thick Evergreens of *Erica-Baccifera*, *Juniper*, and *Cats-Tail*'. Cows, horses and sheep, 'all of a low Size' were bred in Colonsay in Martin's day. Of the human population, Martin described them as 'generally well-proportion'd, and of a black Complexion'. They spoke only Gaelic, were of the Protestant religion, and observed the festivals of Christmas, Easter and Good Friday. The women observed the Festival of the Nativity of the Blessed Virgin.

In 1887 Frances Walker recorded that on Colonsay they 'still hold old year's day, and old Hallowe'en'. There are still parts of the Outer Hebirdes where this is true. At 'Balleraomin Dhu' he visited Kate MacGilvray's cottages, where lived the mother, four children and her two brothers. In a reference to Iain Og Ile, Walker mentions that 'here it was that the late Campbell of Islay, heard from a MacGilvray now dead, his long winded story of the "Knight of the Red Shield",' which is referred to above.

In our own day, the School of Scottish Studies has collected and recorded folklore from Colonsay and Oronsay. They also have a collection of early photographs. Mary Carmichael of Colonsay has been closely involved in preserving local traditions, from several old islanders who, sadly, are no longer with us. Also much involved in collecting local traditions, poems and songs was the late Alasdair MacAllister of Colonsay, who retired to the island after a successful career on the mainland as a schoolteacher and headmaster. It is planned to collate and eventually publish some of the material gathered together by Alasdair.

A more journalistic account of folk culture can be found in the pages of an American MacDuffie. John MacPhee's article for the *New Yorker*, first published in 1969 but republished in 1986 (along with other pieces) as a paperback entitled *In the Highlands and Islands*, is good journalism. MacPhee lived on Colonsay for a while, tracing his own roots, and was a keen observer of island life. Unfortunately, some islanders feel that, having lived among them and been taken into their confidence, he should have been more discreet in what he said. He names names and gives a lot of quite personal detail about people's lives, some of which might have been better left unsaid – at least on this side of the Atlantic.

THE BARD

Amongst Colonsay people themselves, the poet and song-writer most respected is Archibald MacNeill, always known as 'The Bard'. He lived at Riasg Buidhe, the township on the coast north of Scalasaig, abandoned at the end of World War I, when the new houses at Glassard were built. He disapproved of the relocation, and when all the others moved, he stayed put. He lived in the end house, at the north end of Riasg Buie.

Barbara MacAllister Satchel, a native of Colonsay now living in Dunoon, was born in Riasg Buidhe and remembers The Bard – 'he was an old man when I was a girl'. I have to thank her for translating part of one of his songs, about moving from Riasg Buie to Glassard:

Theid thu null leam a Rùin	You will go over with me, my love
's bithidh tigh ùir againn's Ghlasaird,	And we will have a new house in Glassard
'S bho'n tha'n aiteirich cho mòr	And as there will be plenty of time for modern things
Gheibh sinn oran 'san dol seachad,	There will be plenty of time for singing
Chi thu fhein	You will see that they are grand
G'um bheil iad riomhach	Put together with lime and stones
Air an gniomh le aol 'sle clachan Sgleudan tanna Bhailechaolais	The thin slates from Ballachulish
G'an dion bho Ghaoith 'bho fhrasan.	Protecting them from wind and rain.

The locals say that he was a very 'subtle' writer,

and a natural Highland bard. He deserves to be better known.

DONALD MACNEILL

Out of the same mould, though writing in English, is Donald MacNeill of Garvard. He is a sheep farmer who returned to take over his family farm at Garvard, giving up a career as a schoolteacher for the wind, rain and magic of Colonsay. He writes folk songs with lyrical imagery and a 'political' edge, and has had them recorded on tape under the title *Half-Hebridean*. Some of his songs are intensely personal, but others speak of the problems facing Colonsay society in the face of the pressures of modern life:

The winter time, the year grows old,
   first the rain, then the sleet and snow,
numbs the mind with its chilling cold,
   you wonder why you're here.

But then the storm can pass,
   you might see the sun at last,
the sea as still as glass
   the reason then is clear.

You might say that we've made our choice
   we should calm our fears, we should still our voice,
take what we're given and say thanks a lot,
   or they might take it all away.

But what's the use of only standing still,
   soon there'd be nothing here but time to kill,
they've gone so far to make us civilised,
   is this the price we've got to pay?

But what'll we do if today's the day,
   what'll we do if the politicians say:
'We've had enough; it costs too much to let them
                                        live that way;

just let them fade away.'

There is just a touch of bitterness in his song 'We've got it made', where he says:

We're not deprived in the usual sense,
We're doing all right for the pounds and the pence,
We've made a choice and the choice is here,
We've looked to the future and the future disappears.

We've got the freedom to do what we please,
But we've got no freedom at all . . .

SYMINGTON GRIEVE

In the 1920s, Symington Grieve, author of *The Book of Colonsay and Oronsay*, was very interested in folklore and Gaelic culture, although he never approached the level of scholarship evident in the work of Ian Og Ile and Donald MacKinnon. Grieve is the principle proponent of the idea that Colonsay takes its name from Colla Uais, who settled in Colonsay with his brothers in the fourth century AD, according to Irish annals. Dun Cholla is supposed to take its name from Colla Uais, although it is likely to have been built several centuries before that, in the prehistoric Iron Age.

Grieve records the tradition that Colla Uais was descended from the legendary Conn Ceud Chathach – Conn of the Hundred Battles – but even he is forced to admit that for more than six hundred years after the time of Colla Uais the genealogies are patchy and unreliable. This whole area is fraught with difficulties, and perhaps impossible to unravel, but some understanding of what is at stake here can be gained by considering how crucially important it was for the MacDonald Lords of the Isles to legitimate their claims by establishing descent through Somerled's father to the Kings of Dalriada and the High Kings of Ireland.

Symington Grieve's accounts of archaeological monuments on Colonsay and Oronsay are fanciful and unhelpful, especially his discussion and diagrams relating to 'Dun Evan'. The association of Irish epic heroes and Danish kings and princesses with prehistoric forts and standing stones may be interesting folklore, but Grieve makes the mistake of trying to stretch these ideas into historical fact, and his findings make very strange reading from the advantage of today's perspective.

Where Grieve's volumes are extremely valuable is in their recording of local traditions, which otherwise would have been lost. Of particular interest is the story of the demise of Donald Ballach – Spotted Donald.

DONALD THE FACTOR

Donald MacEwan, known in Colonsay as Donald Ballach, was the man appointed factor (estate manager) in 1644 for the Campbells on their newly acquired islands of Colonsay and Oronsay. He resided in Oronsay House. Applying Campbell policies to formerly MacDonald islands, he gained a reputation of being cruel, unjust, and extortionate in his collection of rents.

In desperation the islanders sought help from Colkitto, who had been expelled from Colonsay. Colkitto's youngest son, Angus MacColl Ciotach MacDonald landed at the north end of the island, at Balnahard, with a number of men. He and his followers set off to confront Donald Ballach in Oronsay, travelling by way of Kiloran, Kilchattan, Machrins, Ardskenish and Garvard. At Machrins, on the north side of what is now the golf course, they met a woman in some distress, weeping bitterly. She told Angus that Donald Ballach had taken away her only cow, as *Damph Ursainn*. This is an interesting reference to a custom which must have died out almost everywhere else in Scotland by 1644. Probably introduced by Norsemen, it was a kind of tax which gave a landlord the right, when any tenant died, to the best beast in the widow's stable. If a horse was seized it was called *Each Ursainn*, while if an ox or cow was taken it was *Damph Ursainn*. The word *ursainn* normally refers to door-posts, but in this context the meaning is of a beast being taken out through the door of the byre. Donald Ballach had imposed this tax on the Colonsay widow. He is supposed to have required a share of produce from all the islanders, of butter, eggs, milk, whelks and limpets – all part of the daily diet.

The widow reported to Angus that she had followed the factor's men to the Strand, pleading for the return of her only cow, but they had refused. They were waiting on the Colonsay shore for the tide to go out, so that they could take the beast across to the factor in Oronsay. Angus was outraged by what had happened, and resolved to intervene. He hurried on his way, and met a woman and child further along the track. He asked what clan the child belonged to, and on being told it was a Campbell, Angus drew his sword and cut off the child's head, so worked up was he with rage at the Campbell factor.

At the Strand Angus caught up with the factor's men, who were still waiting for the tide to go out, and forced them to give up the widow's cow, which was then restored to its rightful owner.

Proceeding to Oronsay House, Angus found Donald at home and at his dinner, which consisted of potatoes and seal's meat. Grieve quotes Donald MacNeill of Kilchattan to the effect that when Angus arrived at Oronsay House there was a woman outside grinding grain with a quernstone. The sound had lulled the factor to sleep – perhaps an after-dinner nap – and Angus pushed the woman aside, taking over the grinding of the quern, while he considered his next move. But grinding corn was women's work, at which Angus was unskilled. He ground the stone too hard, making too much noise, and the factor awoke, remarking that the sound was not that of a woman but a man: 'the grinding of a strong man is upon the quern'.

Angus revealed himself, whereupon the factor, realising

that there was no escape, took out his 'sneezin'-mull' (snuff mull) and offered it to Angus with the usual feather for conveying snuff from the mull to the nose. Angus pointed to the feather and asked Donald Ballach if he had many of these. To which Donald replied: 'If I had I would not have waited for you', implying that if he had been feathered like a bird, he would have flown away and avoided capture.

Donald Ballach was seized by Angus and his men, taken to Pairc na h'eaglais, and tied to the stone there – now called MacFie's Stone. Seven of his own men were compelled to shoot him with pistols. He was buried nearby. Apparently Angus avoided legal retribution for his behaviour, the feeling being that the factor got no more than he deserved.

The replacement factor was Colin Campbell, the son of Campbell of Dunstaffnage, who is remembered as a good and prudent man, respected by the local tenantry. He is said to have held the post for three years.

LOCAL TRADITIONS

Grieve records a local traditional belief that there was a battle on the shore at Machrins, north of Dun Gallan, in the reign of David II, possibly shortly before 1369. The story is that some of the local Colonsay MacDuffies fought alongside the men of John, Lord of the Isles, against government forces. Grieve was told by Malcolm Ban MacNeill that the MacDuffies fought with thorn staves – the only weapons available to them. Many were killed and were buried in the sand dunes. Grieve says that 'human bones and portions of metal accoutrements' were often exposed after severe storms, and that local fishermen would not dig for bait on the beach there, for fear of disturbing the dead and so raising a great wind at sea. The Gaelic saying was 'Lagha-chath-na-Sguab air taobh a tuadh Dhunghalin'.

Symington Grieve's book is long out-of-print, so it is worth re-telling some of the stories he collected in order to make them available to a wider public. It is in telling these

197

tales and traditions that he is at his best. His account of the fostering agreement between the MacDuffies of Colonsay and the MacNeills of Barra is of some interest, as some Colonsay MacNeills still claim descent from the Barra MacNeills.

MACDUFFIE STORIES

There are many stories associated with Malcolm MacDuffie who was murdered at the stone at Pairc na h'eaglais in 1623. At the time after 1615 when he was released from prison and allowed to return to Colonsay the island was controlled by Colkitto. Malcolm found it expedient to keep himself hidden, and there are many spots on the islands known as *Leab' fhallaich Mhic a'Phi* – MacPhie's Hiding Place.

The story of MacPhie's black dog refers to events in the life of Murdoch MacDuffie, in the late sixteenth century. This motif is common in Highland folklore and perhaps should not be interpreted too literally. At any rate, Murdoch fell victim to raiding Macleans and was killed at Kiloran Bay by an arrow shot through a hole in the roof of the cave in which he was hiding. He was buried at Oronsay, though his stone cannot now be identified.

MacDuffies and MacFies have spread from Colonsay throughout the whole world. There are Clan MacFie Societies in Australia, New Zealand, Canada and Scotland. The coherence of the MacFie organisations owes a great deal to the research and vision of the late Dr Earle Douglas MacPhee of Vancouver, British Columbia, who collected together and published materials relating to 'The mythology, traditions and history of the MacDhughsith–MacDuffie clan' in 1975.

In Sweden Ulf MacFie Hagman has taken a great interest in clan affairs, and was one of the people involved in re-erecting the MacFie stone. In Scotland Sheila Duffy of Balerno has published a booklet on the MacFies of Colonsay and Oronsay, and there is a small but active organisation promoting research and furthering clan interests. The Lomond and Argyll phone book lists 245 members of the clan and there are smaller numbers scattered throughout Scotland.

There is an active MacFie society in Australia, which publishes a lively newsletter. Many overseas MacFies eventually find their way to Colonsay, to their spiritual home, and pay homage at MacFie's stone to their last chief, descendants of whom still live in Argyll. There is something very touching about meeting these returning exiles: picture an elderly gentleman from Massachusetts and a young doctor from Melbourne meeting on Colonsay – both descended from MacPhies who left the island in the middle of the nineteenth century. There is an appropriate Gaelic proverb:

Cuimhnich air na daoine o'n d'thainig thu
(Remember the men from whom you have sprung).

PIG'S PARADISE

This is a Victorian invention, an inexplicable rendering of the Gaelic place-name *Aoineadh-na-Muc*. An *aoineadh* is a step or ledge between a higher and lower cliff, and this one is the ledge of the pigs. The idea is that it was a place where pigs were kept, and where they could be left without supervision. It lies on the coast to the south-west of Uragaig, and is an extremely dangerous, precipitate spot – not a place for the faint-hearted or for unsupervised children.

HANGMAN'S ROCK

Overlooking the Strand on the Colonsay side is a projecting pointed rock, pierced through, from which criminals used to be hanged. Local tradition has it that most of the people who met their end here were cattle raiders from Islay. It is said that sixteen men from Islay were captured while raiding for cattle and were executed here. There is a marvellous view of the Strand from *Bin-ain-Crom* – the crooked hill – which is reached easily from the shore below.

THE PIBROCH

No discussion of Gaelic culture on Colonsay and Oronsay, however, superficial, could fail to mention Andrew MacNeill of Oronsay. Andrew Oronsay, as he is always known, now lives at Glassard, and has retired from farming. In his day, he was one of Scotland's greatest pipers. Through his teacher Robert Reid, he can trace his mastery of the classical piping music known as the *piobaireachd* or *ceol mor* back to the MacLeods of Raasay and the MacCrimmons of Skye.

The intricacies of Gaelic classical music are debated at great length in the columns of *The Oban Times*. There is a lively and sometimes heated debate about the purity of modern pipe music, as laid down by The Piobaireachd Society. The argument seems to turn on the mental state of Angus MacKay, piper to Queen Victoria. MacKay apparently rewrote traditional pibroch manuscripts in the style of a collection published by the Highland Society of London in 1838. He was an alcoholic, and suffered as well from cerebral syphilis, so his judgement was not unimpaired. His papers eventually came into the possession of Archibald Campbell of Kilberry (1877–1963). In 1947 he published them, but ever since there has been a continuing debate about the authenticity of the pipe settings.

Robert Reid always claimed that manuscripts left by his own teacher, the legendary John MacDougall Gillies of Glendaruel, born in 1854, contained the authentic *ceol mor*. This is a debate which will run and run. Part of the answer may lie in the musical genius of Andrew MacNeill of Oronsay.

11 FACING THE FUTURE

Despite the fears expressed so eloquently by Donald MacNeill of Garvard, Colonsay's future is not as grim as it looked even a few years ago. At the moment the medium-term trends of the tourist industry ensure at least a medium-term future for Colonsay. Under the circumstances, this can only be welcomed.

In the words of Donald MacNeill's song, Colonsay and Oronsay will become 'Half-Hebridean'. There are just not enough young Gaels left to preserve a viable Gaelic community, but with an influx of newcomers, the population is stabilising just above the limit of viability for an isolated island community. It is sad that the islands' Celtic way of life is being diluted, but it shows no signs of dying out, and often the incomers are interested enough in local history and customs to ensure their preservation.

So much depends on the future of Kiloran Estates, and whether the Laird will persevere with his present policies, or sell out to the highest bidder. Other Hebridean islands, notably Raasay, off the Isle of Skye and more recently Gigha, off the coast of Kintyre, have experienced the terrible uncertainty of not knowing who will buy their island, and what their policies will be. Will the newcomers employ the same staff? Will they invest in improvements, look after the gardens around the Big House, allow tourist developments, sell off land for new houses, put the rents up? Will they be pop stars, American businessmen, Arabian princes? When you are so utterly dependent on conditions over which you have absolutely no control, it is bound to have an effect on morale, if not on the social psychology of the island community.

FACING THE FUTURE

Already the island of Oronsay has been sold off, to an absentee American landlord who, fortunately, has taken an interest in the place. But in the cold world of tax-havens and investment trusts, there are no guarantees.

The strain of these kinds of worries can produce their own tensions. Incomers are resented, even though they have brought opportunity to the island, not to mention families to ensure the survival of the school. Traditionalists are resented, for obstructing changes and living in the past. And everybody resents the Laird.

How far these worries apply to Colonsay and Oronsay is a matter of opinion, and of continuing debate, especially in the bar of the Isle of Colonsay Hotel. They are never far away. As long as the island remains entirely in the ownership of one family, they will never go away. Meanwhile, people go about their business, fighting and winning small battles against various Establishments, and trying to be optimistic about their future.

Colonsay has benefitted through expenditure on badly needed infrastructure, especially at the pier and harbour-works at Scalasaig. Road improvements and the provision of mains electricity have also enhanced island life. However, living on an island is not easy. It requires special skills, the capacity for endurance, a sense of humour, a temperament impervious to the insidious effects of unrelenting wind and rain, and a fair amount of personal courage.

Against all this, the islands have a quality of life unmatched anywhere. A Japanese visitor from Tokyo, which has a population over twice that of the whole of Scotland, was ecstatic over his visit to Oronsay. What impressed him most was the *space*, and the fact that when he and his friend arrived on the island, the population increased by fifty per cent! The air is clean, the sea is unpolluted, the drinking water pure. The landscape is beautiful, the sky always changing, the sunsets are out of this world. With a bit of luck, a good dose of enlightenment all round, and sympathetic government, especially in the area of transport policy, Colonsay and Oronsay will survive as living communities.

The worst thing that could happen would be that they were transformed into nature reserves, like the island of Rhum, and became an outdoor laboratory for environmental scientists. But this would surely only happen if the island was already dead as a human community. At the moment there is too much healthy vitality and sheer Hebridean stubbornness for this to be allowed to happen.

James MacDonald, who spent several days on the islands in 1808 while researching his book on a *General View of the Agriculture of the Hebrides*, found his stay there so enjoyable that he temporarily set aside his rather dry, statistical style and went completely over the top in a rapturous panegyric, seeking to inspire future visitors 'with enthusiasm for the grandeur and heartfelt magnificence of nature'. He would tell them:

Gaze on the panorama which a fine day affords [from the summit of Carnan Eoin]. Look around on every hand! Enjoy the view of mountains, seas, and rivers in astonishing variety and contrast! Contemplate the boundless Atlantic and the isles scattered over its bosom, and, when satiated with solitary admiration and delight, return to the elegant, enlightened, and cheerful hospitality of Killoran.

Today the tourist office would give him a job immediately! It is to be hoped that today's visitors are just as happy with their stay.

BIBLIOGRAPHY

Most of the published literature relating to Colonsay and Oronsay is difficult to obtain, being either out of print or inordinately expensive, or in the case of Loder's essential and comprehensive study, both – it is currently fetching over £150 on the secondhand market when available. However, all of the books should be available in a good reference library, or through the inter-library loans system operated by public libraries throughout the world.

Of special importance is the two-volume work by Symington Grieve (1924) which introduced the history and folklore of Colonsay and Oronsay to a wider public. Loder collected together everything about the islands which had some to light by 1935, while the *Inventory* published by the Royal Commission on the Ancient and Historical Monuments of Scotland (1984) is the authoritative reference work for archaeological and historical remains. The book on the Oronsay excavations by Paul Mellars (1987) is important and exciting, but it is written (and priced) for academic specialists. Isabel Grant's book on the Lords of the Isles first published in 1935 but since reprinted, gives a lively, personal view of the history of the Western Isles, and contains some interesting material relating specifically to Colonsay and Oronsay.

Acts of the Lords of the Isles: 1336–1493; edited by Jean Munro and R. W. Munro (Scottish Historical Society, 1986)

Anderson, J., 'Notes on the contents . . . of three shell

mounds on Oronsay', *Proc Soc Antiq Scot*, 32: 298–313 (1898)

Bentley, M. R., Maltman, A. J., Fitches, W. R., 'Colonsay and Islay: a suspect terrane within the Scottish Caledonides', *Geology*, 16: 26–28 (1988)

Campbell, J. F., *Popular Tales of the West Highlands*, 4v (1860–2)

Campbell, Marion, *Argyll: the Enduring Heartland* (Gateway Books, 1977)

Darling, Frank Fraser and Boyd, J. Morton, *The Highlands and Islands*, (Collins, 1969)

Gathorne-Hardy, Alfred Erskine, *My Happy Hunting Grounds* (1914)

Giblin, C., *Irish Franciscan Mission to Scotland: 1619–1646 (1964)*

Grant, I. F., *Highland Folk Ways* (RKP, 1961)

Grant, I. F., *The Lordship of the Isles* (Mercat Press, 1982)

Grieve, Symington, *The Book of Colonsay and Oronsay* 2 vols (Oliver & Boyd, 1923)

Grieve, Symington, *The Great Auk, or Garefowl: its history, archaeology and remains* (1885)

Henderson-Bishop, A., 'An Oronsay shell-mound: a Scottish pre-Neolithic site', *Proc Soc Antiq Scot*, 48: 52–108 (1913)

Loder, J de V., *Colonsay and Oronsay in the Isles of Argyll* (1935)

Jardine, D. C., Clarke, J. and Clarke, P. M. *The Birds of Colonsay and Oronsay: their history and distribution* (1986)

MacDonald, James, *General View of the Agriculture of the Hebrides or Western Isles of Scotland.* . (1811)

McNeill, Murdoch, *Colonsay, its Plants, Climate, Geology* . . . (1910)

McPhee, John, *In the Highlands and Islands* (Faber & Faber 1986)

Maltman, Alex, *A Guide to the Geology of Colonsay* (n.d.)

Martin, M., *A Description of the Western Islands of Scotland* (new ed, 1934)

Mellars, Paul, *Excavations on Oronsay: Prehistoric Human*

BIBLIOGRAPHY

Ecology on a Small Island (Edinburgh University Press, 1987)

Mercer, John, *Hebridean Islands: Colonsay, Gigha, Jura* (Lealt Press, 1982)

Munro, Dean, *Description of the Western Isles of Scotland* (1549)

Murray, Frances, *Summer in the Hebrides* (1887)

Pennant, Thomas, *A Tour in Scotland, and Voyage to the Hebrides* (1776)

Royal Commission on the Ancient and Historical Monuments of Scotland, *Argyll: an Inventory of the Monuments. Vol. 5: Islay, Jura, Colonsay, and Oronsay* (1984)

Shaw, Frances J., *The Northern and Western Islands of Scotland: their Economy and Society in the Seventeenth Century* (John Donald, 1980)

Stephenson, D., *Alasdair MacColla and the Highland Problem in the 17th Century* (John Donald, 1980)

Storrie, Margaret, *Continuity and Change: the Islay, Jura and Colonsay Agricultural Association, 1838–1988* (Oa Press, 1988)

Teignmouth, Lord, *Sketches of the Coasts and Islands of Scotland* (1836)

Walker, John, *The Rev Dr John Walker's Report on the Hebrides of 1764 and 1771*; edited by Margaret M. McKay (John Donald, 1980)

Whitehouse, G. K. *The Wild Goats of Britain and Ireland* (David & Charles, 1972)

Whitow, J. B., *Geology and Scenery in Scotland* (Penguin Books, 1979)

INDEX

INDEX